CHRISTIAN MARRIAGE DEVOTIONAL FOR COUPLES

A 52-WEEK BIBLE STUDY FOR BETTER COMMUNICATION AND A STRONGER CONNECTION WITH YOUR SPOUSE AND GROWING FAMILY

TERI REEVES

HTTPS://TERIREEVESBOOKS.COM/

CONTENTS

A FREE GIFT TO OUR READERS

Claim your copy of "The 5 Most Costly Mistakes To Avoid In Your Christian Marriage" to begin cultivating a God-centered marriage starting now!

Scan the QR code below for access:

To Tony. You came into my life during a time when I didn't know what I needed. God had plans for us, and I thank Him and you for choosing this team. Thank you for always believing in me. My love for you is never-ending.

INTRODUCTION

After an hour-long commute, Jason struggled into the house with a bulging briefcase and an overripe gym bag. Olivia was right behind him with a pile of fifth-grade history essays, a bag of groceries, the dry-cleaning, and their three-year-old, whom she had retrieved from a birthday party.

The house was a cluttered mess: dinner would be carry-out, Jason would retreat to his desk in the corner of the living room, lamenting his recent decision to get his real estate license. Olivia would curl into the corner of the sofa to grade papers, and their son would have the run of the house.

Soon, they'd embark on the bedtime routine, hoping their little guy would stay put for the night; then, Jason would fall asleep worried about finances, while Olivia would stare at the ceiling, wondering about the best way to complete her mile-long check-list before hosting friends the following evening.

There would be no devotional time and no sharing of joys, concerns, or wishes. There might be a short, repetitive prayer, but there definitely wouldn't be any physical intimacy.

Is this your marriage?

Such break-neck, individualized activity void of communication, connection, and consideration of each other's needs, often lands a couple in a counselor's office, or even worse, causes one or both to retreat to an inner world of sorrow and discontent.

And this is hardly a unique situation. After all, each couple consists of two growing individuals who have places to go to, people to meet, projects to accomplish and goals to achieve. They mean well by each other, but can get bogged down with life's daily demands, causing them to lose touch with one another.

Your boss can change your schedule at a moment's notice, or intensify your workload. You might feel pressured to step into more responsibility at church, or attend events for which you have no interest. You may be worried about your future financial stability, or the present need to replace appliances or pay for additional schooling. Perhaps your spouse is crumbling under a load of work, family, ministry, friends, and household obligations, and you'd like to step in, but aren't sure where or how.

Then, there's the children. When to have them? How many to have? And what about when an unexpected one comes along, and expands the family?

You're not alone, and it doesn't have to be this complicated. Many have learned to walk this same path with grace, peace, and unity. All you need is a little insight, a fresh bag of tools, a desire to follow scripture and a determination to enact change.

However, don't let this list of "to-dos" overwhelm you.

You and your spouse have already conquered numerous challenges. You're sharing the same home, various joint accounts, and keys to the family vehicles. You've mastered getting out the door together and socializing as a couple. You know which movies to watch and who wants popcorn and who prefers a bowl of ice cream. You're already doing this thing called marriage. And, although you may be facing new aspects of your relationship, you can be sure to enjoy a life-long return on further investment.

The very best relationships say "I do" every day, and often more than once.

Doing, (taking action), is vital to getting anywhere, whether at home, work, church, or even our neighborhoods. As believers in Christ Jesus, we have the encouragement and direction of God's divine instruction. It provides a basis for doing, instead of just hearing or wishing.

Are you ready to do more to improve upon what you and your spouse have already begun? That's what this book is here to help you accomplish.

Within the pages of this book of devotionals, you'll find 52 weekly studies. Each one offers an applicable scripture, a short inspirational piece, discussion questions, practical applications, and an ending prayer. Now, to get the most out of this book, it's recommended that you:

- Set aside an hour each week, preferably the same day of the week, to read through each topic.
- Work sequentially through the pages.
- Determine which exercise(s) to focus on throughout that week.
- And lastly, take your time.

As we get through the book, we'll cover an entire year of spiritual and practical bits of help that will definitely help you change your everyday life for the better.

This process can also be done as part of a group!

If you choose this option, I highly recommend you allow a short time to greet before each study, offer your guests simple refreshments, and then dive in. Finally, allow an hour or two of group discussion and prayer, to help the members really digest what they've just read and studied.

If you approach the study alone, be sure to share what you're learning with a spiritually mature mentor or friend, as they can offer a listening ear and act as a springboard for ideas. As you begin to implement positive change, you may find your spouse more willing to join in.

While progressing through the book, you'll find tools and insights for growing a God-centered marriage that maximizes your strengths as a couple. You'll learn how to nurture each other and understand each other's needs, as well as better ways to run the household and how to partner for the spiritual well-being of your children. You'll see how intentional living can make a world of difference in all areas of your life.

When I considered writing this book, my thoughts spanned the years of trial and error in my marriage. My husband and I were raised in solid, Christian homes, full of Bible study and prayer, but it took time for us to truly internalize what we saw modeled by our parents.

We read books, attended seminars, and sought godly counsel. And yet, as the Lord began blessing us with children, we found it impossible to remain static in our approach. Who would pay the bills? Who would load the dishwasher? And how would we continue to nurture our marriage, including intimacy, apart from the children?

With the birth of each child, it seemed we started over again in some areas, while others firmly carried us through the transition. We didn't want to lose each other in the hustle and bustle, but most importantly, we didn't want to lose our consistent connection with the Lord.

Soon after, others noted our persistence for a peaceful and unified marriage and came to glean from what we'd learned.

This ignited my passion even more.

I mean, if I could pass along combined decades of marital success from our parents and ourselves, I could expand my mission as a wife, mother, and role model. If I could assist other couples in making growing gains out of growing *pains*, perhaps their lives and marriages could experience greater fulfillment. In this way, as we all became ever-increasing reflections of the Lord's purposes for love, marriage and family, we could breathe new life into an area that is quickly falling prey to busyness and neglect.

Whether you're newlyweds building an initial foundation, preparing your marriage for the arrival of children, or readjusting your focus for your growing family, you'll find practical tips, guidance and inspiration here to help you build a Christ-centered marriage with better communication, and a stronger connection with your spouse and growing family.

Let's get started!

WEEK 1: I GROOM, TAKE THEE, BRIDE

In view of all this, we are making a binding
agreement, putting it in writing, and our
leaders, our Levites and our priests are
affixing their seals to it.

— NEHEMIAH 9:38 NIV

Throughout our lives, we'll make numerous kinds of agreements. They'll range from signing up to bring cupcakes, to taking on a $300,000 mortgage, to pledging ourselves to the one we love. And we'll mean what we say, from the bake sale to the altar, but then come the tests.

In the above passage, Ezra, the priest, was winding up a lengthy ordeal with the children of Israel. They had broken faith with God by disobeying the covenant He made with Abraham, and turned aside to sinful and neglectful pleasures in ways both big and small, so the nation was suffering the consequences. Now, it was time to vow anew. They sorrowfully repented and took immediate corrective action, pledging to follow the rules, regulations, and observances prescribed by God.

We see that Ezra and the people of Israel approached their renewal in four ways. They:

- Voiced their intentions.
- Put them into writing.
- Stood in the presence of witnesses.
- And, finally, they sealed their pledge.

You may notice the similarities between the actions of the Israelites and the progression of events that finalized your marriage. You voiced your love and intentions, signed a marriage license, stood before witnesses to state your vows, then civil authorities affixed their seal.

In ancient Jewish tradition, a copy of the wedding contract is framed and hung in a prominent place in the home. It enumerates the points of the marital agreement, but also the dire consequences of failure.

It may seem strange to post a list of your vows and disciplines for breaking them, but doing so would certainly help to keep the Lord and your spouse at the forefront of your mind, every day.

Plus, in doing this, you will forever cherish the joy, beauty, and excitement of your wedding day. That moment when you said "I do" will linger in your memory for all time. But, it's still the daily "I dos" that cause your love to bloom fully, and your vows to come to fruition. The essence of a godly marriage—the happily working at it ever after—lies in this daily renewal.

As believers in Christ Jesus, you enjoy the same covenantal relationship with God. He gave His promise, kept it throughout the centuries, then renewed it in the person of His Son. His commitment to your eternal good is lavished upon you each day as you walk in the light of His unconditional love.

You can love as He loves, with Christ as your example. Whether you post your vows, or tuck them away in your hearts, you can offer yourselves anew with the assurance that God is with you.

Discussion Questions:

1. How has God shown His love for you?
2. What qualities of Christ do you and your spouse currently exude toward each other?
3. What qualities of Christ do you and your partner need to emulate better to love the way Christ loves you?

Practical Application:

- Read the following verse: "Follow God's example, therefore, as dearly loved children and walk in the way of love, just as Christ loved us and gave himself up for us as a fragrant offering and sacrifice to God." (Ephesians 5:1-2 NIV)

- Describe the love Christ has for us. How can you love your spouse in this way?
- Catch each other loving as Christ loves!

Prayer:

Dear Lord, help me renew my vows of love and commitment to my spouse each and every day. Help me become more like You in my marriage, so that my spouse sees You in me. Amen.

WEEK 2: COMMUNICATION IS KEY

*To answer before listening—that is folly and
shame.*

— PROVERBS 18:13 NIV

In the first chapters of Genesis, we encounter the dynamic
conversations between God, Adam and Eve. God asks a question, and Adam answers. God asks more questions of Adam and
Eve and gets direct responses each time. There's a clear understanding of thoughts, words and deeds.

However, there's another speaker in chapter three—Satan. His
words sought to twist and deceive, to produce confusion and a
devastating outcome.

The conversations between God, Adam and Eve were honest, although sorrowful. The exchange between Satan and Eve was full of half-truths and misunderstandings, which ushered in the fall of humanity.

Today's passage speaks of answering before hearing or listening. In the example of Genesis, we see that God listened. He didn't make assumptions, but instead asked questions, and listened for replies before speaking again. He's our supreme example.

When you listen to your partner, actively participate. Many times, this means setting aside your devices or stopping to engage in eye contact. If you're unsure of what they're speaking of, or why they may be using a specific tone, just ask. Jumping to conclusions before your spouse has fully explained themselves can lead to unnecessary arguments. And, when you ask questions, do so to gain an understanding, not to undermine or interrogate the other person.

Ephesians 4:29 warns against unwholesome talk and encourages us to speak about what helps us build each other up according to the needs of the listener. You can achieve this even when discussing troublesome topics, if you choose words, tones and body language that seek to build instead of overpower or gain the upper hand in the argument.

Speech that is unwholesome tears down the listener, inviting tears, anger, and resentment. Whereas wholesome speech uplifts and produces peace.

Stop to consider what is motivating a particular conversation, and whether you truly wish to be understood in the end, or just win an argument. Choose wholesome words to avoid unintended outcomes. Whether you're communicating a need, simply sharing schedules, or planning a date night—communication is vital.

Philippians 4:8 instructs us to concentrate on thoughts that are true, noble, right, pure, lovely, admirable, excellent, or praiseworthy. If we make an effort to keep these factors in mind, speech, and practice, then our interactions will be peaceful and productive.

Think back to the dialogues in Genesis. Desire understanding and truth. Never engage your spouse in order to discourage, take revenge, or deceive.

Discussion Questions:

1. Reflect on the scriptures above. What does God want you to understand about communication? Was there a time when you weren't fully present as your partner tried to communicate with you?

2. What are some ways you can increase positive communication with your spouse? How often do you sit down with your spouse to casually speak to each other?

Practical Application:

- Read James 3:3-5 (NIV): "When we put bits into the mouths of horses to make them obey us, we can turn the whole animal. Or take ships as an example. Although they are so large and are driven by strong winds, they are steered by a very small rudder wherever the pilot wants to go. Likewise, the tongue is a small part of the body, but it makes great boasts. Consider what a great forest is set on fire by a small spark."
- Using the metaphors of a horse, ship, and spark, what do you think God is telling us here about the power of our tongue (Crump, 2013)?

Prayer:

Heavenly Father, please guide the words I use when speaking to my spouse. I pray for improved and more effective communication in our marriage. May Your Holy Spirit guide us to approach and respond to each other with love, grace, and understanding. Amen.

WEEK 3: HERE COMES THE BABY!

Every good and perfect gift is from above,
coming down from the Father of the
heavenly lights, who does not change like
shifting shadows.

— JAMES 1:17 NIV

Many of the gifts we give and receive turn out to be less than perfect, because we, as humans, are imperfect. But, when we receive a gift from God, we can be sure it's a top-of-the-line treasure. As couples united by the Lord, our first treasure rolls over and looks at us each morning. He or she is cherished in the heart, whether or not they look like treasure at 5:00 am! And, since God is a gift-giver by nature, He often cannot stop at just one.

In other words: here comes the baby!

Only, this time, rolling over at 5:00 am may turn into a rare occurrence, as your new, little treasure may wake you a few hours earlier, and maybe even several times each night. During this process, all your insecurities may also come up to downplay your joy.

However, just as your first "I do" was a beautiful proclamation of love, and you've been figuring it out daily, the "we're pregnant" can work just the same. No one knows exactly what to expect when uniting with their partner, just as there are unknowns when birthing and raising a child. However, humankind has proven its willingness to embark on both journeys with hopeful mystery. The main thing to remember is that, in giving you a child, God is always adding, never taking away.

Continue with your couple's devotions and prayer. Sit together and talk, as you always have. Watch your favorite movies still, and pursue fellowship with friends. One of the worst mistakes new parents can make is to isolate themselves due to all the tiredness. True, a newborn will need lots of time and attention —you're all that little guy or gal has to keep them going—but if you split chores, errands, cooking, or picking up take out, neither of you will shoulder the full impact of the transition.

2 Corinthians 3:4-5 reminds us that our confidence is from the Lord, and that we are not called to be competent in ourselves. No one knows precisely how to be a parent until they face

parenthood. Every day, and through every stage of a child's growth, you continue to grow right along with them. Some points of your baby's care will come surprisingly naturally, and some will take research and prayer, but you can be sure the Lord desires for you to receive His gift with joy and greater dependence upon Him.

Remember, your child is a bonus blessing to your relationship. Adjustments will need to come, of course, but make them prayerfully and with the advice of godly parenting pros. Look upon your child with grateful hearts, and know that God has a purpose for each and every one of you. Your baby will help fulfill the plan for you as an individual and a couple; you, in return, will be blessed to help mold and fashion a precious treasure for God's glory.

Discussion Questions:

1. How is God moving in your marriage right now?
2. Describe the following: how has your relationship with your spouse changed since becoming pregnant or having children?

Practical Application:

- Read Psalm 5:11-12 (NIV): "But let all who take refuge in you be glad; let them ever sing for joy. Spread your protection over them, that those who love your name may rejoice in you. Surely, Lord, you bless the righteous; you surround them with your favor as with a shield."

- Discuss the ways you and your spouse will rely on God more this week.

Prayer:

Dear Father, thank You for giving my spouse and me the precious gift of a child. I pray that You fill our marriage with love, and help us rely on You for continued strength and wisdom, so we can nurture our gracious gift from You. Amen.

WEEK 4: HANDLING CONFLICT CHRIST'S WAY

... then make my joy complete by being like-
minded, having the same love, being one in
spirit and of one mind. Do nothing out of
selfish ambition or vain conceit. Rather, in
humility value others above yourselves, not
looking to your own interests but each of
you to the interests of the others.

— PHILIPPIANS 2:2-4 NIV

Conflict. It's going to happen.

A pastor friend of mine once said he wouldn't marry a couple unless they'd already made it through some "knock-down, drag-out fights." Of course, he was only joking, but learning how to get through an argument with grace and resolution is a biblical art.

Most conflicts spring from within.

One partner thinks one way, and the other opposes. Opinions can fly like daggers and pierce the heart of the one you love. In the above scripture, we're admonished to be united with one purpose and look to the interests of others. This applies to all relationships. If we can view our spouse as a brother or sister in Christ, not just our marital partner, we may be able to approach conflict with a greater emphasis on scriptural obedience.

When you place your partner's interests above your own, it will help you to better understand their perspective. Don't hesitate to ask questions, in order to understand their reasoning or desires. Also, be ultimately willing to sacrifice your point of view to live in godliness and holiness, which is a much higher calling than happiness.

Times of conflict provide a learning opportunity for greater emotional and spiritual intimacy. If you attempt to avoid them at all costs, you will stunt the growth of your relationship. Conversely, if you see every disagreement as a call to arms, you may injure that very closeness you desire.

When it's needful to engage in conflict, make sure you know what God's Word says about the subject. Thoughtfully share the scripture with your spouse, and pray that the Holy Spirit guides you in its application. The goal is never to win, but to live according to God's will for His children and your marriage.

Proverbs 27:17 (NIV) says: "As iron sharpens iron, so one person sharpens another." This verse easily applies to husbands and wives. A bit of friction caused by conflict can sharpen a couple's focus and understanding.

Now, there are 5 distinct love languages: words of affirmation, receiving gifts, acts of service, quality time and physical touch (Chapman, 1995) . Study your partner: which of these do they show or embody? Knowing their love language may help you improve your approach when serious discussions are warranted.

When's the best time to approach them for meaningful conversations—according to their needs? When's the best time for you? Do you need to settle your emotions through prayer first, perhaps take a few minutes outdoors, or wait until after dinner? No one wants to face a possible disagreement when tired, hungry, in need of a fresh shower, or after a long commute.

If the Word seems unclear, or you can't find a precise solution within its pages, consult with a spiritually mature family member or friend—if you both agree to do so. And, share only what's necessary, without incriminating your partner.

Discussion Questions:

1. What does conflict look like in your marriage? Hurt feelings? Passive-aggressive behaviors?
2. When in conflict, do you use sarcasm to communicate with your spouse or make questionable comments?
3. As a couple, are you open to conflict, or do you view it as a threat (Focus on the Family, 2016)?

Practical Application:

- Take the following quiz to learn your partner's personality type and love language. Record the results and refer to them often https://www.5lovelanguages.com/quizzes/

Prayer:

Dear Lord, please help us hear each other and Your Word whenever we face conflict. May our marriage reflect Christ's love even as we sharpen one another. Amen.

WEEK 5: CONNECTING WITH YOUR SPOUSE—SPIRITUAL INTIMACY

He humbled you, causing you to hunger and
then feeding you with manna, which
neither you nor your ancestors had known,
to teach you that man does not live on
bread alone but on every word that comes
from the mouth of the Lord.

— DEUTERONOMY 8:3 NIV

Spiritual intimacy stems from Bible study, prayer, and worshipping together. When a couple shares a biblical worldview and operates according to the same standard of Scripture, they can enjoy sweet communion of the soul. And, with a strong foundation of spiritual intimacy, all other types of intimacy have a greater chance of growing to maturity as a result.

When the children of Israel went wandering through the desert, they grumbled and complained whenever their physical bodies experienced hunger. They would accuse God and Moses of neglecting their appetites. However, their greater need was to follow the Lord and obey His commands. That was the *true* source of life.

If a couple concentrates on physical unity and satisfaction as their top priority, they will soon find something missing. The same problem occurs if they focus on financial success, recreational enjoyment, or even starting a family. Living by the Word of God is primary to all else in a stable marriage.

While growing in spiritual intimacy may present a challenge, especially during busy seasons of life, it can be steadily achieved with a bit of pre-planning.

Now, this is important too: Don't get bogged down by comparing your devotional or worship times with other couples. Take it at your own pace. Schedule just one night a week to look into the Word together and pray—as you're doing now. You may also want to keep a prayer and praise journal as you watch the Lord work in your individual lives and marriage —this will help you recall what you've been through, as well as what God has previously done for you.

Decide which church services you'll attend and who's on nursery duty from week to week, but stay in service together whenever possible. Sing together, rejoice in the supportive atmosphere of other believers, take notes during the sermon and share your thoughts on the way home or over lunch. Nugget of wisdom: this is not a time to critique the pastor, but to communicate what the Lord impressed upon your heart during the time of teaching. This will ensure you get the most out of your Sunday message, while also providing an opportunity to grow in spiritual intimacy with your spouse.

You can also play Christian music at home to invigorate your mind with uplifting words. It's a great companion at dinner, and it encourages your soul while tidying up or engaging in conversation.

The Word of God is food for our innermost beings. When you and your spouse are on the same spiritual diet, you can grow together throughout the years with a strong spiritual bond (Squires, 2016).

If you have children in the house, include them in devotions, as appropriate, and set aside prayer times for the whole family. However, never neglect those quiet moments of sharing a Psalm, whispering heartfelt prayers, and giving thanks to God for each other in private.

Discussion Questions:

1. Who has been the most influential in shaping your spiritual walk with God?

2. How often do you and your spouse take intentional time to cultivate your spiritual intimacy?

3. In what ways have you helped your spouse become more spiritually mature?

Practical Application:

- Building spiritual intimacy takes time. Devote a few moments, at least one day a week, for tending to your spirituality with your partner. This may mean attending a church service every Sunday, attending a Bible study, reading the Bible, or simply praying together.

Prayer:

Father God, I pray that our relationship be built on a solid spiritual foundation. Please give us wisdom, time, and the resources to nurture our spiritual intimacy, so our unity may grow stronger, day by day. Amen.

WEEK 6: CONNECTING WITH YOUR SPOUSE—EMOTIONAL INTIMACY

The man said, "This is now bone of my bones
and flesh of my flesh; she shall be called
'woman,' for she was taken out of man.

— GENESIS 2:23 NIV

When two people share their experiences, past and present, including accompanying thoughts and feelings, they're experiencing emotional intimacy. When they identify with each other's feelings, their emotional intimacy can grow exponentially. But before this can happen, each must agree to become vulnerable before the other.

It's easier to communicate the facts of the day, or recount childhood stories as concrete happenings, without expressing the thoughts and feelings connected with them. This may seem like a logical way to communicate, but it merely touches upon the intellectual side of things, and not the emotional. Imagine the disconnection that would occur between a couple, if he just said what he did that day, and she shared what she did that day, period. You've communicated, sure, but only as much as you would with a customer service clerk!

Next, imagine listening to your partner vent about a challenging day at work, and the subsequent exhausting commute home, while you just stare, wide-eyed, without any kind of interaction. This is much like listening to the evening news—there is no feedback, and only one active participant.

Ultimately, both husband and wife want to be heard, responded to, and understood. But, if either is locked up emotionally, an essential part of intimacy will be lacking, which will result in one or both feeling like an outsider.

Now, on a related topic, many say women are better at self-expression in all its forms, and perhaps this has a historical reason. Since biblical times, it was women who were tasked with gathering at the well each day. No doubt, they met up with female friends from the surrounding villages and talked about daily life. Then, as mothers, they provided much of the verbal stimulation given to their babies—thus passing along language.

However, if we stop here, we'll miss an important truth:

While the women gathered at the well, the men also met—at the city gate. Here, they had valuable conversations about ethics and the human condition, among other things. They listened to community news and judged arguments between villagers. This means that both men and women have played integral parts in their communities since the beginning of time, and in order to fulfill their roles, they engaged in meaningful, and many times emotional, exchanges.

When a husband and wife share their thoughts and feelings, they offer an open door for each other to help shepherd their emotions. Sometimes, seeing things from the other's perspective can defuse a situation at work, or provide advice about a complicated matter with extended family or friends.

Confiding in your spouse will often result in unified prayer or a plan of action to embark upon together. It may also prompt a warm hug and a shoulder to cry on: all of which are equally important.

If either of you finds emotional vulnerability difficult, just practice doing it a bit at a time. Share deeply, as your spouse listens and offers their support without judgment or recommendation. Be honest in the presence of your bride or groom. Revisit your love languages to pick up more clues that can help you deepen your emotional intimacy.

Discussion Questions:

1. Describe the ways you feel loved. Then, ask your partner how you can do a better job of communicating love to them.

2. In what ways do you feel your spouse's unconditional love?

3. How do you respond when romantic feelings come and go?

Practical Application:

- Affirm your partner and pay them compliments daily.
- Discuss implementing a daily sharing time to expand your emotional intimacy.

Prayer:

Father God, please help me be more vulnerable when sharing with my spouse. Help me express my honest emotions so our marriage can grow in intimacy. Amen.

WEEK 7: THE SECRET TO MAINTAINING GREAT PHYSICAL INTIMACY

May your fountain be blessed, and may you rejoice in the wife of your youth. A loving doe, a graceful deer—may her breasts satisfy you always, may you ever be intoxicated with her love.

— PROVERBS 5:18-19 NIV

She slides into bed, hoping he's already asleep, and cuddles up with her favorite, fuzzy blanket. The baby's in the next room, and their toddler's down the hall. Yes, he's asleep. Once again, she skirted the issue of physical intimacy. She wanted to be close, as in the past, but the path to lovemaking has too many obstacles.

First, they became new parents, and the learning curve exhausted them both. Plus, her stretch marks and tummy bulge brought secret tears when catching sight of herself in the mirror, and he had worked overtime to cover for maternity leave and felt underappreciated. They struggled through and reconnected, but then baby number-two arrived.

By then, they knew they had to get serious about life in the bedroom, or they'd make a habit out of the disconnect, and face a multitude of negative consequences as a result.

Does this sound familiar?

It doesn't have to be this way. Remember, between you and your partner is a life-giving marriage born from the ultimate giver of life and love—God. He wants you and your spouse to be connected: mentally, emotionally, spiritually, and physically.

Most new moms do not feel as sensual or attractive as they did before having a baby. They gain weight, their bodies take on a different shape, and their hormones rage as they go through the process of re-regulating. They're unhappy about these changes and feel less desirable to their husbands, and most importantly, themselves.

Most husbands understand these changes and accept them as her contribution and sacrifice to carry their child. Some men will even see the mother of their children as an extension of their ego and be more affectionate than ever.

During this time of many changes, however, it's *essential* to reconnect with God first: To lean into Him through prayer and daily devotions. To pour out your heart and accept His unconditional love.

You see, your worth never changes in His eyes, and He loves without conditions or expectations. When you're passionate about God's love, you can offer yourself anew to your partner in a more understanding way.

Don't forget that physical intimacy can also mean holding hands, exchanging warm embraces, or snuggling up on the sofa. It can also be a foot massage or sitting closely (Squires, 2016).

In Proverbs, God instructs men to take pleasure in their wives. Husbands, you can help your wife accept your physical advances by assisting her in self-acceptance through God's love. Wives, you can be sure that a husband who's connected intimately with God will also be able to connect with you.

Discussion Questions:

1. What makes your partner feel desired? (If you don't know, ask!)
2. Can you put forth greater effort to provide these things?
3. Think about God's unconditional love and acceptance of you. Does this change the way you see your partner? Or the way you see yourself?

4. Is there anything about your lovemaking you think
   could be improved?

Practical Application:

- Commit to rehearsing the prayer below, and sharing
  yourselves intimately and freely, at least one day of the
  week. As your passion for God and your spouse grows,
  you can then increase the frequency.

Prayer:

Dear Father in Heaven, please open our eyes to Your unwavering and endless love for us. Help us love and serve You more, and love and cherish each other the way You do. Help us be more intentional about creating love and passion within our marriage. Amen.

WEEK 8: COMBINING DIFFERENT DISCIPLINE AND PARENTING STYLES

Listen, my son, to your father's instruction
and do not forsake your mother's teaching.
They are a garland to grace your head and
a chain to adorn your neck.

— PROVERBS 1:8-9 NIV

When you look upon your newborn child, so many hopes and dreams flood your heart and mind. If you could choose a world of peace, equity, love, and success for them, you would surely do so. But, while you're dreaming your will for your baby, your spouse may have different ideas and ways to achieve them. When these ideas represent differing parenting styles, it's back to the drawing board for unity.

Discipline styles come and go: from spanking, to standing in the corner, to getting a "naughty chair," to no physical discipline at all—just grounding the child from what they enjoy.

Then, on the other end of the spectrum, there's letting the child have everything: from high-dollar allowances, and the freedom to run with any available friend, to everyone staying home and receiving only the basics.

One of the problems with these shifting styles of discipline is that none truly represent the timeless instruction of God's Word. God is love, and His ways are merciful and just: not just one or the other. And, He is a God of order—sameness. We may even say, predictable! He directs the way and rewards, or disciplines us, as we go.

Your spouse may have different methods of instructing or disciplining, but the main objective is to know what he or she is trying to achieve. Do you agree that the final outcome is to raise a child that knows, loves, and obeys the Word of God? Or is it something else? If it's just to prove that you're a better parent than your folks, or if your style is all about not wanting your children to make the same mistakes you did, then that's not necessarily a scriptural motivation.

Because of this, parenting is another facet of marriage that calls for unity and compromise: this is crucial in order to nurture your relationship with your spouse and your child. Both parents must agree to keep the Scriptures as the definitive source for right and wrong, and for how to handle discipline issues.

Here's a good example of this concept in action: suppose your child lies, and mom communicates her sadness, shares the scripture concerning lying, and prays with the child. Then, dad takes the child to the neighbor for confession. Such working together for the same result, but with different roles or methods, communicates unity to all. And yet, a prayer, along with time of scriptural instruction with both parents, will ultimately have the best effect.

When disagreements in how to handle discipline arise, keep the conversation private. Search the Scriptures and pray first in unity, and *then* approach your child or children.

Discussion Questions:

1. What are some parenting principles you've learned from the Bible (Pugh, 2017)?
2. How do you incorporate biblical principles into your parenting (Pugh, 2017)?
3. How is your household like a mini-church for your children (Pugh, 2017)?
4. What challenges of discipline did your parents encounter?

Practical Application:

- Read Deuteronomy 6:2 (NIV): "so that you, your children and their children after them may fear the Lord your God as long as you live by keeping all his decrees and commands that I give you, and so that you may enjoy long life."
- Discuss the following: how does a parent's love for God flow through to their children?

Prayer:

Father in Heaven, we come to You asking for Your guidance in parenting our children through Your Word. May we align together to parent with Your Holy unity. Amen.

WEEK 9: COMPLETING THE HOUSEHOLD CHORES TOGETHER

You may ask me for anything in my name,
and I will do it. If you love me, keep my
commands. And I will ask the Father, and
he will give you another advocate to help
you and be with you forever.

— JOHN 14:14-16 NIV

In the above passage, Jesus says we can ask anything in His name, and He will do it.

We may think this only applies to critical matters such as health, financial issues, or maybe a relationship that needs mending. But, as believers in Christ, we can actually ask for *anything* according to the Father's will, and receive it. We can be sure He hears our cries for help—even with something as "small" as household chores.

And, on that topic: the traditional roles of who does what chores have changed by necessity in recent years. Fewer women are housewives nowadays, (and if we're being honest, they never were). No one is married to the house these days; instead, everyone plays the role of a homemaker, including husbands. Just as it takes two to form a marriage and birth children, so does it take both parties to keep the household running smoothly. This is even more true as the family expands.

Who does what at home should be a topic of ongoing discussion, so things can run smoothly in the household. A weekly family meeting may help clarify areas needing improvement, or additional tasks for a specific time and season, for example. Herein lies another opportunity to know your spouse. Are they okay with dishes left in the sink overnight, or vacuuming every other day? Is it agreeable to do deep cleaning only a few times each year?

When your children are old enough to take on small responsibilities, add them to the family chore team and assign age-appropriate tasks, such as helping to set and clear the table. Older children can dust, vacuum, take out the garbage, and load the dishwasher.

And, this part is important: Always be willing to adjust tasks for the best outcome.

For example: if your spouse finds they dislike rinsing the dishes, but enjoy doing the laundry, feel free to switch things up! Another example: suppose one of you had an exhausting week—in that case, feel free to trade chores to accommodate energy levels.

The main thing to remember when keeping the house neat and tidy, is that everyone lives there. Everyone adds to the disarray, but just as much so, everyone can also pitch in to help the house run more smoothly.

At times, you may even need to ask the Lord for help—and this is perfectly fine. He may need to move upon your spouse or children to do their part. As we serve one another, always remember, we are also serving Him.

Discussion Questions:

1. What are some chores you don't mind leaving undone for a couple of hours or even a day?
2. Are there any responsibilities you can assign to one of your older children?
3. Are there responsibilities you would like additional help with from your spouse?
4. What is your understanding of the biblical roles of husbands and wives (Focus on the Family, 2016)?

Practical Application:

- Pick a day of the week and speak with your spouse and older children (it's okay if they are not old enough to participate yet).
- Create two lists. One list will be non-negotiable household chores that must get done within the week, and the other, the tasks both you and your spouse are okay putting off.
- Create a schedule for the non-negotiable chores.
- Then, feel free to substitute the negotiable ones for some alone time with your partner, or maybe some quality family time.

Prayer:

Thank You, God, for showing us the example of what it means to be an obedient and humble servant, as Your Son Jesus Christ. We pray that together we can serve each other and our family in tangible ways. Please guide us as we continue to maintain the home You've given us. Amen.

WEEK 10: OVERCOMING THE GUILT OF NOT WANTING ANOTHER CHILD

Therefore, there is now no condemnation to those who are in Christ Jesus, because through Christ Jesus the law of the Spirit who gives life has set you free from the law of sin and death. For what the law was powerless to do because it was weakened by the flesh, God did by sending his own Son in the likeness of sinful flesh to be a sin offering. And so He condemned sin in the flesh, in order that the righteous requirement of the law might be fully met in us, who do not live according to the flesh but according to the Spirit.

— ROMANS 8:1-4 NIV

Life doesn't always go as planned.

It brings its surprises, both joyful and otherwise, leaving us to figure out our next steps. Consider, for example, a young wife learning of her fourth pregnancy: she stares at the home pregnancy test as its "positive" indicator hits her with the force of a typhoon. She would never terminate the child the Lord has blessed her with, but she doesn't feel the same kind of excitement and awe as she did with her previous children. She's disappointed, fearful, and wondering how she'll even manage. Then comes the guilt and shame of her joyless response.

"Mom-guilt" is very real.

It might be that she was starting a new chapter in her career or ministry, or that she doubts her ability to divide her love and care among more children. She may have just lost the weight from her previous pregnancy, and was feeling energized, or her past pregnancies may have presented health risks she hoped to never again repeat. Whatever the reason, pregnancy can bring a very lonely and helpless feeling to a mother - especially if the rest of the family are thrilled with the incoming addition.

Some women birth a child or two and feel they're not able to handle another pregnancy. They may dread the physical and mental exhaustion of starting the process all over. They may feel emotionally spent, and so decide to choose how large their family will become in agreement with their spouse.

In both cases, the mother dearly loves the children the Lord has already given her, but adding on more brings feelings of overwhelm. And, this is important: God understands. This is when a couple should approach His throne of mercy with heartfelt prayer.

He will not condemn either partner for feelings of guilt, shame, or regret, because He's a God of healing and forward motion. You can take any negative thoughts or concerns to Him and leave them there. Then prayers for wisdom, discernment, and peace can be used to guide you in your next steps.

If God blesses you with an unexpected pregnancy, you can be sure it's no surprise to Him, and He has a perfect plan for everyone concerned.

If you need help determining the number of children that's best for your family, ask the Lord. He's very willing to come alongside your marriage to instruct, assure, and comfort you and your partner. With His all-knowing love, He can turn that guilt into grace, fear into faith, and anxiety into awe. As His children, you can entrust yourself and your family size into His capable hands.

Discussion Questions:

1. How have life's circumstances or goals changed for you and your spouse since having children?
2. Reassess your life at this moment: what does it look like moving forward with your current children? What

joys do you feel when you imagine the future as it is (Regalo, 2020)?

3. The decision to have children is very impactful. How can you support your spouse if feelings of shame and guilt arise regarding having another child (Regalo, 2020)?

Practical Application:

- Read John 3:17 (NIV): "For God did not send his Son into the world to condemn the world, but to save the world through him."
- Discuss this scripture with your partner. What are God's redemptive purposes and desires for you?

Prayer:

Dear Lord, I confess my sins today and pray You cleanse my mind, body and soul, so that I can cast away guilt. Help me understand Your perfect love in every situation, and to look to You through all of the uncertain times I face. Amen.

WEEK 11: COMMUNICATE THE WORD OF GOD TO YOUR CHILDREN

Hear, O Israel: The Lord our God, the Lord is one. Love the Lord your God with all your heart and with all your soul and with all your strength. These commandments that I give you today are to be on your hearts. Impress them on your children. Talk about them when you sit at home and when you walk along the road, when you lie down and when you get up.

— DEUTERONOMY 6:4-7 NIV

Imagine if we could know the exact number of words we speak to our children each day. Imagine, again, if we knew how many of those words, phrases, and sentences contained scripture or godly inference.

The above passage instructs us to incorporate training in God's commands throughout the entire day. Such instruction is most readily accepted in small bites—and, even better, communicated by *example*.

When your children wake up each morning, thank God for the new day, the songs of birds, and the good night's sleep, as you help your children make their beds. Say things like: "The Lord is so good to give us another beautiful day!"

When you sit down for breakfast, give thanks, and ask the Lord for guidance that day. Then, share one biblical virtue with your children as they eat.

When you ride in the car or take a walk in the neighborhood, note God's wonders in creation and communicate His will for humanity.

Before bedtime, do a quick "blessing session."

Ask each of your children to name one blessing they received that day, and one the Lord helped them give to someone else. Accept every answer from: "I'm thankful for ice cream after dinner," to "I picked up my brother's socks!" It's an excellent time to remind them of God's commands about servitude, and making the interests of others as significant as our own.

However, as your children grow, they may resist hearing about God in every aspect of their day—you may need to get clever. You can speak to your spouse, in your child's hearing, about the things of the Lord, without addressing your son or daughter directly.

As parents, you know your children love to overhear parental conversations and interject as they see fit. Allow them to join in and use the opportunity to impart God's wisdom.

Proverbs 13:10 says that wisdom is found in those who take advice. If you take God's advice first, you'll be able to better communicate and model it for your children, and children that have developed trust in your listening ear and counsel will continue to listen as they grow older.

With today's busy schedules, it isn't easy to connect with your children as much as you may like, but rest assured that the Lord meets your efforts to share His Word and instruct your children in the way they should go.

Discussion Questions:

1. What are some ways your family helped reveal the Word of God to you when you were growing up?
2. What activities can you do together as a family while sharing the Word of God?

Practical Application:

- Set aside a few minutes each evening to develop a family routine incorporating the Word of God. This may be inviting the whole family to complete chores, having them help make dinner, or simply taking a walk.
- Whatever the activity, do it as a family and include God's wisdom.

Prayer:

Dear God, we pray that You bestow Your infinite wisdom into our hearts and souls, so we may pass it onto our children. Please help us teach our children, and guide them in the way of Your commands. Amen.

WEEK 12: SETTING HEALTHY BOUNDARIES WITH EXTENDED FAMILY

Even if I caused you sorrow by my letter, I do not regret it. Though I did regret it—I see that my letter hurt you, but only for a little while—yet now I am happy, not because you were made sorry, but because your sorrow led you to repentance. For you became sorrowful as God intended and so were not harmed in any way by us.

— 2 CORINTHIANS 7:8-9 NIV

The moment you become husband and wife, the world changes.

You're no longer available to everyone at any time, and your privacy becomes a top priority. When you add your first baby, life changes again, and so on with each subsequent child. Setting biblical boundaries is a healthy way to protect what the Lord has established for your marriage and growing family.

That said, not everyone will agree with the safeguards you establish.

Sometimes, they have no personal boundaries themselves, and see yours as an object of pride or division. Yet, don't let this discourage you: Those who can't respect and embrace your guidelines don't do so out of conceit or strife against you, but because they lack the habits themselves, and thus, they can't understand how important they are.

Many times, your loved ones will be on different levels of spirituality, or not even live in a basic, daily walk with the Lord. If this is the case, then allowing their harmful worldly habits and vices to infiltrate your marriage will only lead to constant struggles between you and your spouse.

And here's the issue: Many of our extended family members often feel like it's their right or responsibility to interfere and advise.

They may argue their case against your boundaries, calling them unnecessary, exclusive, or demeaning, but the heart of the matter lies in their rejection of biblical obedience, not in your setting of healthy boundaries. They resent the Lord's wisdom and instruction, placing their relationships with you above your relationship with God and your spouse.

When you direct those who oppose you to scripture, you allow them to see the reason behind your actions as being part of your walk with God, not a personal affront. It's up to them to accept the root of your boundaries, or continue to focus on their fleshly objections.

However, make every effort to back all boundaries with scripture, and reference each passage, when explaining them to your extended family and friends. They cannot be responsible for what they don't know, and the best way to walk in authority to protect your family is to give prominence to the Lord's will.

Once the wisdom of God is brought into the picture, it will be clear that your boundaries spring from your obedience to Christ, not from any personal dislike of others. Be bold, yet loving, as you choose God's will over pleasing family and friends. It may produce a few awkward moments, even hurt and anger, for a time. However, it will ultimately invite further discussions about a biblical lifestyle—which inevitably leads to growth and blessings for both sides.

Discussion Questions:

1. What are some boundaries you want to establish for your household? Discuss them with your partner.
2. Talk about why these boundaries are necessary, as you continue to grow in spiritual connection.
3. What outcome are you hoping for by setting these boundaries? Do these outcomes honor God?

Practical Application:

- Together with your spouse, list your physical, mental, and spiritual limits. Discuss what you can tolerate, and what makes you uncomfortable. These feelings will help you discover your limits.
- As you continue the work of connecting spiritually, tune into your feelings, and when those limits arise, communicate them to your spouse.
- Be willing to present these limits to the person(s) that necessitated the setting of a particular boundary.

Prayer:

Dear Lord, please help us define and establish boundaries in our marriage, according to Your Word, and give us the necessary boldness, consistency and wisdom to share them lovingly and respectfully. Amen.

WEEK 13: BUILDING A GOD-CENTERED MARRIAGE COMMUNITY

*They devoted themselves to the apostles'
teaching and to fellowship, to the breaking
of bread and to prayer. Everyone was filled
with awe at the many wonders and signs
performed by the apostles. All the believers
were together and had everything in
common. They sold property and
possessions to give to anyone who had
need. Every day they continued to meet
together in the temple courts. They broke
bread in their homes and ate together with
glad and sincere hearts, praising God and
enjoying the favor of all the people. And
the Lord added to their number daily those
who were being saved.*

— ACTS 2:42-47 NIV

From the Garden of Eden, God designed His children to live and grow in community—as couples. He explicitly fashioned Eve to be Adam's helper and blessed their union. But, He didn't stop there! It was never His will for any of His children to live in isolation or loneliness, so He built a kingdom of believers to assist each other along the pathways of life.

The early church exemplified sharing, unity, and protection. To be within this God-ordained group was to enjoy the safety and comfort of other brothers and sisters, which undoubtedly enriched individual marriages.

God provides each of us with loving and firm support from family and friends; they accompany us through adversity and celebration. Think of your particular circle: you can probably name the roles of each one. Who's the prayer warrior? Who's the helping hand? The best athlete, the most encouraging, or the most in need?

You can learn God-focused lessons from the stories of every couple in your group, and each has something to contribute to your marital growth and reliance upon the Lord. In fact, you may already function in your role as a couple, or be in the process of figuring it out with the help of your family in the Lord.

However, beware of this: although a God-centered marriage community can be a bolstering pillar and a healing balm, it can also become fertile ground for comparison and critique. Every couple must guard their hearts against discontent with their husband or wife, as they witness positive qualities in other couples which are not yet present in their own marriages. The same goes for gifts, talents, job status, ministry, intelligence, looks and experiences the Lord might've given to someone else.

All in all, the Lord unites according to the needs of the group. Ask Him to add as He knows best. Be willing to accept newcomers and rally together, as each couple, in turn, draws upon the strength of the group—which is crucial during any life transition. The whole team can tackle new jobs, new babies, a change of residence, a health issue, or any spiritual needs.

Know who's in your cheering section too: support one another as the early believers did, banding together for the highest good of all.

Discussion Questions:

1. What does the Bible say about having a community?
2. Think about other couples/friends. How can you form a God-centered community with them?
3. How has your community helped strengthen your marriage?
4. What is your role and purpose in your marriage

community? What gifts and experiences do you bring
to the table?

Practical Application:

- Read Proverbs 27:9 (NIV): "Perfume and incense bring
  joy to the heart, and the pleasantness of a friend
  springs from their heartfelt advice."
- Discuss the benefits of having a friendship in which
  both individuals seek God.

Prayer:

Dear God, we pray that unity prevails in our community. Use us
as Your instruments to help build a God-serving circle of
married couples. Help us unite our experiences so we can listen,
learn and support one another. Amen.

WEEK 14: CARING FOR YOUR RELATIONSHIP WHILE CAREGIVING FOR A FAMILY MEMBER

The King will reply, 'Truly I tell you, whatever
you did for one of the least of these
brothers and sisters of mine, you did
for me.

— MATTHEW 25:40 NIV

Caregiving has many forms.

It can be assisting a family member after an injury or surgery, or providing long-term care for an elderly and ailing parent. But it also means the care you give to your spouse and children.

It's imperative to realize that your marriage is a caregiving relationship, and takes priority over all other care agreements. This doesn't mean you refuse to help family members in need of assistance, but that you evaluate your time, energy, finances, and lifestyle to see what sacrifices are feasible, and which would be detrimental. And, lastly, you and your spouse must both realize that taking care of another will also incur an emotional toll.

You may need time to coordinate medical care, insurances, and your loved one's financial affairs. You may not have the physical strength to perform direct-care duties, such as bathing and toileting, and you may feel emotionally overloaded depending on the verbal demands of the one for which you're caring. These particulars can overwhelm your marriage and family, or expand your teamwork and experience.

Whenever a need for specialized care arises, have a family meeting with extended members to divide tasks as much as possible. Although you and your spouse may have willing hearts and sensitive spirits, discuss the big picture, to help keep all aspects in order.

Ten ways to keep your marriage strong while extending care are:

1. Making prayer a daily priority.
2. Searching the Word for answers and encouragement concerning your situation.
3. Continuing to worship and seek fellowship with brothers and sisters in the Lord.
4. Reevaluating and splitting household chores.

5. Taking turns providing care and companionship to your loved one.
6. Enlisting friends and family to give you respite for a night out.
7. Maintaining your social schedule as much as possible.
8. Keeping your bedtime routine.
9. Making memories with your loved one as a couple.
10. Thanking God for the opportunity to serve together.

Most of all, be sure that caregiving, in each particular circumstance, is the Lord's will for you and your spouse—you must be in complete agreement here. Ask your spiritual leaders for input and support before making your decision, and always have an exit plan. Not everyone can care for a declining loved one for an indefinite amount of time. Be sensible, realistic, and willing to adjust as time goes by.

Guard your marriage with a high wall of protection, yet spread forth your arms and gather in the needy—into the *outer* court.

Discussion Questions:

1. How can caregiving in marriage affect one's choice for employment and recreation?
2. What limits, if any, should couples place on the workload they choose to accept when caring for a loved one?

Practical Application:

- Read Psalm 121:1-2 (NIV): "I lift up my eyes to the mountains—where does my help come from? My help comes from the Lord, the Maker of heaven and earth."
- Discuss a time when God has given you strength during a moment of uncertainty and weakness.

Prayer:

Heavenly Father, help us remember that we're here to serve others as if we were serving You. Please give us patience and compassion as we reach out to others, and lighten our burden so we can nurture our marriage in the process. Amen.

WEEK 15: PRIORITIZING TIME FOR REST AND SLEEP

*Come to me, all you who are weary and
burdened, and I will give you rest. Take
my yoke upon you and learn from me, for
I am gentle and humble in heart, and you
will find rest for your souls. For my yoke is
easy and my burden is light.*

— MATTHEW 11:28-30 NIV

Is it possible to be filled to the brim with both joy and exhaustion?

Ask any new parent, and they'll give an affirmative nod. How can such a tiny, helpless little bundle demand so much from his or her parents? Precisely because they're tiny and helpless!

A newborn's parents are their only guarantee of survival, and there's more to it than snuggles, eating, and diaper changing. There's bathing, shopping for a different brand of diaper (if the stockpile you pre-purchased doesn't agree with your baby's skin), calls to all-pro parents about this rash or that blotch, and figuring out how to trim delicate fingernails while the baby is sleeping—among many other things.

Thus, as you can see, your sweet newborn actually becomes a big family project!

Because of this, you'll find yourself falling asleep during movie night, or just skipping it altogether to grab a few hours of sleep by stealth. If you just make some pre-baby agreements with your partner, however, you'll find you can navigate this area much easier.

Decide what chores can go without doing, and for how long. Ask a close friend or family member to come sit with the baby a couple of afternoons a week, so mom can get a warm shower or a soaking bath. This way, she can be fresh when her husband gets home and feel a bit more like herself, and hubby can rest after his workday. Make simple, do-ahead-and-freeze meals that can heat quickly, so the dinner dilemma isn't a nightly occurrence for a few months.

And, most importantly: relax.

Jesus invites you to come to Him when tired and weary. It doesn't matter what caused the tiredness or weariness; He's always available to provide rest. He doesn't promise a rest from the work itself, but rest and refreshment while going through it, and also, of course, afterward.

He wants you to yoke up beside Him.

A yoke is a wooden collar used to join two animals together—usually oxen—to split the load of pulling a cart or farm implement. Together, they get the job done with equal effort (Mowczko, 2010).

Now, imagine being yoked to Jesus. He desires for you to work alongside Him in His work, so that He may lighten your load.

Remember that Jesus called the children to Himself and blessed them. He knows what it takes to oversee these masterpieces of God's creation!

You can sleep when the baby sleeps, eat after the baby eats, and take turns on diaper and bathing duty while mom regains her stamina, day by day. And, never forget, Jesus is always just a whisper away. Call out to Him whenever you feel emotionally or physically overwhelmed—He's always ready with a gentle and humble heart to give you rest.

Discussion Questions:

1. How does this passage help you think differently about your current situation?

2. What are some ways in which you can share the responsibility of your work with the Lord?

3. Think about your partner: how can you help share the burden of their workload as Jesus would?

Practical Application:

- Work out a schedule with your partner to split your duties, allowing each of you to alternate and care for your little one, as ready and well-rested as you can.

Prayer:

Dear Lord, we ask for Your strength to fall upon us. Teach us how to work together and rest our burdens with You, so we may not grow tired and weary. Amen.

WEEK 16: SPIRITUAL SELF-CARE

Very early in the morning, while it was still
dark, Jesus got up, left the house and went
off to a solitary place, where he prayed.

— MARK 1:35 NIV

Setting aside quiet times with the Lord isn't always easy.

The demands of your everyday life will do their best to crowd Him out. Why? The answer is simple: our fallen society and selves do not naturally cling to God.

Consider an avid jogger.

Each morning, they get up and look out at the big, wide world, and to whatever the weather has to offer that day. Then, they have to make a choice: will they defeat all physical and emotional urges to move forward without their run, or will they overcome resistance and follow through? No doubt, many distractions are calling their name, and even true-blue runners must fight to conquer all the reasons their minds will provide to stay inside.

Spiritual self-care is much the same.

And, do keep in mind, the reasons to skip it will add up as you have children. However, your soul still needs that spiritual nourishment from the Lord, just as much as you need to eat or drink. Because of this, it's vital that you and your spouse put down every thought that tells you you don't have the time, energy, or wakefulness to sit quietly before the Lord in prayer.

In the above scripture, Jesus got up before dawn and left the house to find a solitary place to pray. His actions here were very intentional: you see, He had to get up before anyone could engage with Him, before distractions and resistance could present themselves; leave, and seek the Father.

Proper self-care begins and ends with God. He knows every detail of our beings and every care of our lives; if anyone knows just what we need and when—it's Him.

Some married couples mistakenly believe that all quiet time should be spent together. They also mistakenly look to their spouse for strengthening that can only come from the Lord. Such thinking can be very dangerous, as it puts our spiritual health solely in the hands of our partner, and this can prove to be devastating, as they're not equipped to supply all of our needs —only God is.

Therefore, don't feel guilty about taking time for just you and the Lord. Jesus did, and He's our supreme example. If He needed that quiet time of connection, then certainly, we do even more.

Remember, all relationships take time to build; this is the same with the Lord. Just as you plan for marriage-building moments and activities, so must you make time to engage with your Heavenly Father. And, as believing spouses, you should desire the same God-only getaways for your husband or wife, as this can only ultimately benefit your marriage and home as a whole.

Any time spent in Bible study, prayer, quiet meditation or worship will benefit your marriage and family. It's in observing proper spiritual self-care that we actually observe our spiritual family care.

And, hear me out here: you don't need to go on a three-day retreat to achieve this necessary refreshment and strengthening of the spirit—just engage in a consistent habit of spending time with God. However, if such extended times do work for the whole family, they really can produce amazing and positive experiences with the Lord.

Ultimately, you should think of what's most sustainable for you. Perhaps fifteen minutes a few times a week, then fifteen minutes every day. Share what the Lord shows you in your quiet times to make your spiritual self-care a blessing to everyone in your home!

Discussion Questions:

1. How many times in the last week have you sat quietly alone to pray, read the Word, or just spend time with God?
2. What keeps you from practicing spiritual self-care, and spending quality time with God? Does it come from saying 'yes' to everyone, all the time? Do you experience feelings of guilt when taking time for yourself?
3. In what ways can you glorify God with self-care?
4. What can you do to create space and freedom for your partner to spend more time with God?

Practical Application:

- Plan a time at least one day this week, to free your partner up for 15 minutes for some much-needed personal time with God. You can then increase the time, as feasible.

Prayer:

Father God, I pray that You renew my mind, body and soul as I glorify You, by taking intentional time to sit quietly in Your presence. Amen.

WEEK 17: DISCUSSIONS ABOUT MONEY AND FINANCES

And my God will meet all your needs
according to the riches of his glory in
Christ Jesus.

— PHILIPPIANS 4:19 NIV

In this week's passage, Paul declared a blessing of the Lord on the Philippian church. They had given him a generous offering, and he received it with gratitude. However, Paul met any and every circumstance with contentment—even financial hardship.

How can you face the days ahead with the same confidence?

It is really only possible when seeking the kingdom of God. It is then, in that walk with God, that we can be sure we'll receive all that we need. Paul's life is an example of putting God first and, as a result, being cared for accordingly.

When you put God first, you'll become more secure in His will and provision for you, and this includes family size. Children are our most precious gifts from God, and He knows what's needed to nurture and nourish them. You may need a larger home or car, or maybe more money for living expenses, but rest assured: He's ahead of you, making the way in every area.

Furthermore, adding a child or two doesn't need to be an occasion for fear. Instead, it's an opportunity to walk in greater faith as the Lord uses various means to draw you closer to Him. Growing your family could actually be the catalyst to your spiritual maturity!

God is always faithful.

He knows your every need, and has met them all throughout the years. He won't stop now just because your family is growing. In fact, He's actually in the very middle of all that growth, as He *is* the Life-giver, and from whom all good gifts come.

To boost your faith in this area, spend time with other families that have blazed the parenting trail and learned to lean on the provision of the Lord; they can help you plan and pray, but also walk before you as living proof that God does indeed take care of His own.

Paul learned the secret to being content; he knew God would supply all that he needed. He kept his focus on fulfilling God's will for his life, and God focused on providing for Paul. Such a glorious partnership made everything work as it was supposed to.

Never forget that each child the Lord adds to your family is a gift. He knew the child before you held him or her in your arms, and He knew what was needed not only by that child, but every other member of your family. He knew what a blessing each child would be to your marriage.

Keep your eyes on the Giver, and be thankful for the myriad of blessings He sends your way. Meditate on His riches in glory in Christ Jesus. It all belongs to Him, and so do you and your growing family.

Discussion Questions:

1. Discuss 1-2 early memories about money you have from your childhood (Baumer et al.,).
2. What level of importance do you think money plays in your life (Baumer et al.,)?
3. What concerns do you have about finances and taking care of your family?

Practical Application:

- Together with your spouse, make a list of the five most

significant concerns you have about money, finances, and the family.

- Select one of the answers from your list and discuss ways God has already provided in that area.
- Discuss a time when provision didn't come how or when you wanted it, but it all worked out even better than you'd hoped.

Prayer:

Heavenly Father, we ask for Your financial blessings to continue to flow into our lives. We have faith that You will always provide for each member of our family. Amen.

WEEK 18: RAISING A CHILD WITH SPECIAL NEEDS

*The Lord said to him, 'Who gave human
beings their mouths? Who makes them
deaf or mute? Who gives them sight or
makes them blind? Is it not I, the Lord?'*

— EXODUS 4:11 NIV

The most crucial focus of the birth of any child surrounds the gift of life.

Every newborn has a specific hair and eye color, length of fingers and toes, but those are only secondary to their beating heart. How miraculous it is to hold your little one close and experience the sights, sounds, and even scents of a newly born baby.

But, what if your little bundle comes with a few surprises?

Sometimes, birth disorders are seen right away, and at others, they're only revealed after a complete medical checkup, or a difficulty in functioning. Whatever the case, such challenges do not need to diminish the wonder of life itself.

Imagine all the special needs of a helpless seven or eight-pound human: they are entirely dependent upon knowledgeable and willing parents to remain alive even in their first few hours. Because of this, even more so, a child in need of greater care opens the doors for parents to become critically dependent upon God.

In the passage from Exodus, we see God revealing a portion of His mysterious creative character: it is He who creates disabilities. He doesn't say why, but He's content to take the credit.

In Psalm 139:13-16 (NIV), we see that life begins in the mother's womb, and is watched over and formed by the hand of God. And God makes no mistakes: He intentionally pre-arranges the purposes for every living soul.

A child purposefully formed with special needs may call upon parents to do things a bit differently.

You may need to research a particular disorder and learn specialized techniques for feeding, or how to operate certain medical equipment. You may have extra implements in your diaper bag, or need to keep your little one home for safety and health reasons.

When giving birth to a child with special needs, remember the disability of *sin* in each one of us, and how God fathers us with love, care, and mercy, despite that. As you serve your little one, remember to serve as unto the Lord, with the grace and mercy of Jesus.

We don't always see the Lord's reality, but as we trust that unseen realities are more real than what's humanly discerned, we can grow immensely in our walk with God.

Yet, in all the extra care and concern for a child with special needs, *do not neglect yourself or your spouse.* Share the load with the Lord, and be sure neither of you is left to figure it out all alone. Live your faith while caring for your child's disabilities; your self-sacrifice is an example of Christ's selfless love to all who are watching.

Be examples of unity, endurance, and ever-growing dependency on the Lord, as you care for each other and your precious newborn. Keep your eyes on the goodness of God, and your arms ready to reach out to one another.

Discussion Questions:

1. In what ways has God provided for you in your times of greatest need?

2. How has God revealed that your caregiving is a reflection of His love and care for you?

Practical Application:

* Read Psalm 31 (NIV) together with your partner. Reflect upon this passage. Remember that, as the parents of a child with special needs, you are called to live in harmony and peace with one another. Have patience with yourselves and each other, even when you do not get it in return.

Prayer:

Heavenly Father, we lift up all our children's needs to You. Help us remain faithful and to see the good through every challenge, knowing and recognizing that we are Your marvelous creations. Amen.

WEEK 19: CLINGING TO FAITH WITH AN UNFAITHFUL PARTNER

> *Let love and faithfulness never leave you; bind*
> *them around your neck, write them on the*
> *tablet of your heart. Then you will win*
> *favor and a good name in the sight of God*
> *and man. Trust in the Lord with all of*
> *your heart and lean not on your own*
> *understanding.*
>
> — PROVERBS 3:3-5 NIV

God designed marriage as a union between one man and one woman for life. Then, He instituted regulations overseeing their relationship to protect them in body, soul, and spirit.

When a husband and wife embrace God's lordship in their marriage, they and their future generations can experience the lasting joy afforded by obedience. That said, however: obedience doesn't necessarily guarantee worldly happiness or continuous euphoric intimacy.

Couples enter dangerous waters when they turn their gaze from Christ and allow the temptations of the world to capture their focus. The enemy knows that, if he can distract, he can eventually lure. And once in his trap, all of life is painfully affected.

Infidelity in a Christian marriage is usually a gradual process.

The husband or wife becomes emotionally bonded with another man or woman, drawing them away from their own spouse. Studies show the most common arenas for this occurrence are in the workplace, and also, in fields of ministry.

As their sharing deepens, the enemy springs into action, suggesting more intense ways to cement their illegitimate bond. And whether or not the two engage in romantic and sexual expressions, marital trust is already broken.

Infidelity can be emotional, sexual, or even financial. It simply involves drifting apart from your spouse, creating bonds, and making decisions as if you were single.

The pain of unfaithfulness isolates the offended partner, and can easily lead to depression and lack of self-worth. The only way to remedy this is to cling to the Lord for solace and healing.

Outsiders, though well-meaning, may sometimes direct people away from Christ, the church, or even their spouses. What should you do in these trying circumstances, then?

First, wait upon the Lord for guidance.

Speak with Him about your fears, anger, and frustrations. He will then gently lead you to either forgive your spouse... or to move away from the relationship altogether.

Either way it goes, the road will undoubtedly be rough. Because of this, your connection to Him will remain critical for you, your children, and your extended family and friends throughout the entire process.

Infidelity will not break you if you cling to the Father, and in a marital relationship, you can really cling only for yourself. You can't force your partner to choose God—they have to do that on their own. If they don't, then remember that a break came between your spouse and God, before it did between your spouse and you.

When individuals remain close to God, they will remain faithful to their marriages and families. The world will always beckon, and the enemy will always roar, but a couple that leans into God first will be kept safe.

Discussion Questions:

1. How have external trials, in the past, helped make your marriage stronger?
2. In what ways were lifelong commitments modeled in your family during your childhood?
3. What do you think it means to center your marriage in Christ?
4. How do you handle difficult situations? Do you take them in stride, or do you allow them to consume you (Focus on the Family, 2016)?

Practical Application:

- Read 1 Peter 4:12 (NIV): "Dear friends, do not be surprised at the fiery ordeal that has come on you to test you, as though something strange were happening to you."
- Discuss the importance of seeking faith and strength in Jesus Christ through all types of adversity (Focus on the Family, 2016).

Prayer:

Dear Lord, thank You for always being faithful to me. Please help me remember that, although others may betray me, You are always with me. I pray for the restoration of our faithful union. Amen.

WEEK 20: SUPPORTING YOUR SPOUSE

Therefore encourage one another and build
each other up, just as in fact you are doing.

— 1 THESSALONIANS 5:11 NIV

How wonderful it is to be supported by our all-knowing, all-loving, and all-capable Heavenly Father. He never leaves us stranded with troubles or looks away when we're tired, frustrated, or in need of wisdom.

And He never wants us to be alone.

From the times of the Garden of Eden, He brought woman alongside man to dispel loneliness, and to share in the work of bringing life to the earth. Furthermore, in God's perfect plan, a married couple is united to Him, as well as to each other.

Because of this, encouragement in matrimony is supposed to be rich and ongoing. Plus, when you add in brothers and sisters in Christ Jesus, everyone is built and uplifted.

The apostle Paul commanded us to support one another like this as we, as a community of believers, await the day of Christ's return. He knew the pitfalls of loneliness, and the everyday battles, threatening to divide, discourage, and destroy us—which the enemy often does through isolation.

It's the same within marriages.

If either spouse is left to uplift and encourage themselves through the trials and temptations of life, he or she may become worn and dismayed. This is especially true as the couple is blessed with children.

Going back to the Garden, we see God's desire for ongoing communion between Himself and His creation. And, although He provides the primary support for both man and woman, marriage was designed for *mutual* edification.

Just as the woman was brought to the man as a helper (Genesis 2:18), she, as the weaker vessel (1 Peter 3:7), needs his help. A God-focused interdependency has been the Father's perfect plan all along.

Think of the ways you support your spouse as an individual.

You care for them as you do yourself, you desire them to have good health, rest, and fulfilling work, wholesome relationships with friends and family, and most of all, an ever-growing walk with the Lord. Because of this, you're willing to do your part to support the achievement of these things and more.

Now, add in the children.

Your spouse still has the exact same needs, but now they're intensified, and perhaps a bit harder to meet. Your little one will demand much time and attention from sheer necessity, so supporting your spouse may call for you to be a bit creative after having children.

The key here is to regularly seek the Lord together in prayer, and encourage one another with a short Bible verse that offers inspiration and praise. Rejoice together when blessings come your way, and listen when things don't turn out as planned.

Even with God as all-caring and all-supporting, you should be your partner's biggest fan, and loudest cheerleader—their most fervent prayer partner, and most willing advocate and defender.

Support can be a shoulder, a hand, a leg-up, or a reminder to sit back and relax for a while. It can be reading the Psalms aloud when your partner is worried or anxious, or taking a drive together down a country road.

After all, laughing, crying, struggling, and achieving are best done with the support of the one whom you've pledged your love and life to.

Discussion Questions:

1. In what ways does your spouse support you in your marriage and with the family?
2. How has your spouse's support helped you see Christ in them?
3. How does God feel about the way you're supporting His child (your spouse)?

Practical Application:

- Write a list of five ways your partner provides support to you and the family.
- Talk about ways you feel encouraged by their support.

Prayer:

Dear Lord, please help me encourage my spouse the way You encourage me. Please give me the discernment to serve my partner as Your son or daughter. Amen.

WEEK 21: BEING SELFLESS FOR YOUR SPOUSE

...not looking to your own interests, but each of
you to the interests of the others.

— PHILIPPIANS 2:4 NIV

Do you know what interests your spouse?

Some things are apparent, but many may go unspoken as your husband or wife grows and changes throughout your marriage.

A new job, new baby, or a change in fellowship circles can change your partner's needs, wants, and interests. Because of this, continuing to unify through the changes can keep your relationship fresh and vibrant.

The above passage speaks of looking not only to your own interests, but to the interests of others. Such awareness is achieved through humility, and lived through self-sacrifice.

Suppose your spouse has interests contrary to your own, or ones that are inconvenient, or which force you from your comfort zone. We aren't speaking of sinful habits or things that would divide your family—just things that are more "him" or "her" than they are you. Are you able to set yourself aside as needed?

The conflict comes when one partner is willing to, and does so regularly, while the other does not extend the same grace or preferential treatment. Yet, to give way to the one you love is a way to communicate their importance!

Also, notice that the above passage speaks of others—plural.

This refers to the body of Christ in general, which certainly includes your believing spouse, and its instruction should be practiced first and foremost in your marriage.

However, if you're continuously being called upon to give place to the interests of others, how will your needs and desires be met? Well, one way can be by a spouse who shares your obedience to the Word of God, as well as a community of believers that functions according to the example of Christ.

And yet, giving preferential treatment to your spouse and to others doesn't mean to forgo all legitimate needs and wishes you have of your own. Practicing self-care glorifies God for the life He's given, and exercising your gifts glorifies the Holy Spirit who gave them to you—and sets an example.

Children raised to be aware of the interests of their parents and siblings will take that awareness out to others as ambassadors of God's love and salvation.

A God-centered marriage can include a fun-loving contest of who considers the other more first and selflessly—a contest where both win, and children can learn to recognize the value of promoting the needs of others.

"Where do you want to go to dinner, dear?"

"Wherever you want, love."

"But, let's go where you want."

"It's ok—we went where I wanted to go last time."

Love prefers the other. It watches for opportunities to serve, sacrifice and bless.

Discussion Questions:

1. Ask yourself: how can I become more selfless in our marriage?
2. Together, read Ephesians 5:25-32. What connection do you see between the selflessness in marriage, and Christ's sacrifice on the cross? Compare this verse with

serving your spouse unconditionally, by laying down your life the way Jesus did.

3. What is one thing you enjoy that you wish your partner would do with you?

4. Ask your partner what you have done or could do to make them feel more loved.

5. Talk about a time you felt God called you to do something uncomfortable. How did you feel once you completed the task?

Practical Application:

- Commit to doing something you may not find enjoyable. Be selfless by "laying down" your comfort for your spouse, focusing on the benefits that doing this can bring to your marriage, as well as for your efforts to be more like Jesus in everyday life.

Prayer:

Father God, please help me put the needs of my spouse and family before my own, looking to You for wisdom and strength to give importance to others, without sacrificing my own well-being in the process. Amen.

WEEK 22: CONTENTMENT, NEVER COMPARISON

> *Am I now trying to win the approval of human beings, or of God? Or am I trying to please people? If I were still trying to please people, I would not be a servant of Christ.*
>
> — GALATIANS 1:10 NIV

You've heard the catchphrase: "You do you."

Although these three simple words can give applause and approval to ungodly living, they also carry a ring of biblical truth.

In Galatians 1:10, Paul speaks of living a life that pleases God, not people. He's not interested in temporal, human acceptance, but eternal approval as a servant of the Lord.

In growing your marriage and family, it's critical to accept the Lord's plan for who you are, where you live, what you own, and how you will serve Him.

There was only one Apostle Paul, one John, one Martha, and one Dorcas.

Each of these Biblical personalities had different missions in the body of Christ, and each performed them as unto the Lord —not men.

You as well, as an individual, and as a married couple, have a God-given purpose for the days and times He has placed you. Because of this, it's essential to know your spiritual gifts and to put them to work within the Kingdom of God—never comparing your gifts and ministries to others, but giving thanks for your own.

Imagine if the heroes of scripture sat in comparison and envied one another. Would the fruit of their labors nourish us now?

Imagine a young mother, comparing her looks, energy, or birthing and parenting experience with thousands of other mothers on social media: scrolling through page after page of content and images, all declaring her as "less than" the rest.

Or maybe a couple who envies the home, jobs, income level, or opportunities of other couples, but rarely gives thanks for their own.

In all cases, we are rendered ineffective to our families, friends and the body of Christ when we stop to compare, complain and crumble beneath the weight of our own envy.

Psalm 37:4 speaks of delighting in the Lord, so He may give you the desires of your heart. You cannot delight in Facebook, Twitter and Instagram, expecting to walk away with all of your desires fulfilled. This is only possible when you focus on the Lord, being grateful for His plans and designs for you, your marriage, and your growing family.

Develop a habit of thankfulness, keeping your thoughts centered on God's goodness and love. Speak of His blessings all around, and the unique ways He has gifted your family, spiritually and materially.

Life is an adventure when you curiously look for Him each day, and celebrate His one-of-a-kind relationship with you and your spouse. "Do you" His way, and you'll become the best you ever— one too grateful to be anything else.

Discussion Questions:

1. What are some harmful effects of comparing yourself and your marriage to others?

2. What accomplishments can you point to in your
    marriage and family that make you proud?
3. Read 2 Corinthians 10:12. Why, according to God, is
    comparing ourselves to others not in our best interest?
    What does Paul say about comparison?
4. Read Hebrews 13:5. What does this passage say about
    the root of contentment? Where do you get your
    contentment from?

Practical Application:

- Practice gratitude! Together with your spouse and
  kids, make a list of 10 things you're grateful for in your
  marriage and family.

Prayer:

Father God, it is easy to compare our marriage and family to
others, but we pray that You help us keep our eyes on You.
Please help us accept Your will for us and to receive each other
with all of our imperfections. Amen.

WEEK 23: DON'T COMPETE, BUT COMPLETE, YOUR SPOUSE

If a house is divided against itself, that house cannot stand.

— MARK 3:25 NIV

Have you ever felt like you were competing with your spouse?

A marriage with two people who function like enemies, in a constant battle of wits or skills, is not a safe one; not for the husband, the wife, or the children.

In the above passage in Mark, we see Jesus explaining that if He used the devil's power to cast away demons, Satan's kingdom would not stand. Satan would gain nothing by allowing Jesus to use satanic power to destroy his own work.

The purposes of Jesus withstood temporary disruptions by the betrayals of Peter and Judas, but only for the more excellent plan. However, if the members of the Trinity worked against each other, it would only create an unparalleled disaster. Jesus' attitude toward the Father prohibited such rivalry, but engaging in it was Satan's downfall.

Within marriage, we see the union of two creations of God: a partnership called to complete each other through thoughtful and selfless service. Though husband and wife retain God-given roles, they're also brother and sister in the Lord. When both roles are recognized and complemented, there is no room for competition.

There are endless scenarios that can give way to a battle of words, deeds, and decisions. When these arguments happen in front of the children, they learn to show disrespect, as modeled by either parent.

Moms and dads will not always agree on the best ways to discipline a child, or on what privileges or possessions are approved. This is when calm discussions and mutual agreements should occur in private before presenting them to the child.

However, at times, you'll need to respect your partner's on-the-spot opinion even though you disagree. Be patient and willing to hear your spouse's reasoning later, when you're away from the child's hearing.

God created marriage as the union of a husband and wife who forsake all others to maintain a God-centered relationship (Genesis 2:24). He made each unique, yet with a unified purpose that completes a bigger picture.

Think of the many positive traits shared between you and your spouse—of the weaker areas that can be strengthened by the other. None of these are reasons to compete, or worse yet, to destroy your house, but to build for the good of your entire family.

The body of Christ Jesus has many members, each with different gifts and callings, yet all of the same importance. Form the habit of seeing your spouse in the light of their gift. When you see their role in the body, you may see their contribution to the unity of your marriage more clearly.

Rejoice in your uniqueness, and recognize your partner's strengths in places you may be weak. Celebrate the perfecting power of Jesus Christ as you grow into maturity and turn aside from competition.

Discussion Questions:

1. Have you experienced, or do you currently sense, competition between you and your spouse? If so, how does this make you feel?

2. When disagreeing with your spouse, do you aim to

"win," or glorify the Lord by working together as a couple?

3. How does Ephesians 5:28-30 go against competitions within marriage? What would be the outcome if members (parts) of your body started competing against one another?

Practical Application:

- The next time you and your spouse disagree, practice compromising, rather than competing, to win with your side of the argument.

Prayer:

Heavenly Father, I pray that You unify my partner and me to raise our kids to know the importance of working together and glorifying You, O Lord. Amen.

WEEK 24: FLEXIBILITY IN MARRIAGE AND PARENTING

As Jesus walked beside the Sea of Galilee, he saw Simon and his brother Andrew casting a net into the lake, for they were fishermen. "Come, follow me," Jesus said, "and I will send you out to fish for people." At once they left their nets and followed him.

— MARK 1:16-18 NIV

Simon and Andrew were going about their business as fishermen when Jesus walked by and changed their lives. Scripture doesn't record the details of their story, but we can imagine the trust it took to walk away from their livelihoods in favor of an unknown path.

If someone else had called them to leave their nets, their story could have ended in disaster. But we, looking on, know their faith and courage were in good hands.

How flexible are you when the Lord asks you to change directions?

Sometimes, this comes as a new job opportunity, or the chance to participate in a challenging ministry. But, more so, He beckons us to bend and flex within our marriages and come away from habits and ways of thinking that do not serve unity. However, whatever is too rigid to bend, will often break.

Being flexible with what you do and how you do it gives room for the Lord to make life-giving adjustments. If He can rearrange your schedule and add or subtract from your "to do" list, you'll find your delight in Him, rather than in your own methods and achievements.

Sometimes, the Lord will stretch you to what appears to be your outer limits, then provide you with respite, as well as eyes to see what He was after. Within parenting, He may call you to ease back and wait at times where you'd rather pounce, or to speak up at others where you'd usually remain silent. He may give greater insight into the needs of a particular child, so you may modify the way you guide them.

Likewise, within marriage, He's always ready to help you improve your approach to both difficulties and celebrations.

Yes, sometimes we need a better grip on acknowledging our spouse's victories just as much as we zero in on problems!

However, flexibility also extends to those beyond your home. That new family on the block, that teenager at church, or the landscaper that comes to mow your lawn—they can all represent heavenly connections.

A life of trust in God, and His orchestration of events, is one of the most exciting aspects of the Christian walk.

When He goes right, we go right, and when He goes left, we go left too, as He directs. We stop as He commands us to, and go forth with His favor. As you lay your plans before Him, pause and give Him room to tweak them as He wills. Remember that your marriage is always a partnership of three.

Discussion Questions:

1. How do you incorporate flexibility into your marriage, or in your relationships with your children? What about relationships with your extended family or church members (Krejcir, 2003)?
2. What happens to your relationship with God, and the gifts God gave you, if you only consider your own ideas or plans (Krejcir, 2003)?
3. Are you experiencing challenges or issues in your parenting or marriage that could improve if you were a little more flexible?

Practical Application:

- Talk with your spouse about times both of you have been flexible and inflexible in marriage and parenting. Brainstorm possible solutions and ways both of you can exhibit more flexibility in your relationship.

Prayer:

Father God, builder of all things, I pray that You help us be more pliable to Your words, and glorify You. Empower us to live according to the plans You have for our marriage and family. Amen.

WEEK 25: SETTING GREAT, (AND REALISTIC), EXPECTATIONS

Yes, my soul, find rest in God; my hope comes from him.

— PSALM 62:5 NIV

When you first contemplated marriage, which expectations came to mind?

The basic ones should be a commitment to faithfulness, honesty, open communication, regular employment, putting together a household, worshipping and laboring with other Christians, and maybe the two-year plan for your first child.

A more detailed outlook might include a division of household duties, parameters for work hours, who does the shopping, and who pays the bills.

These essential components in the basic line-up are all part of God's plan for unity and purity within a marriage.

Matthew 5:27-28 is clear about adultery and lusting with the eyes. Colossians 3:9 speaks about honesty. Ephesians 4:15 advises us to speak the truth in love—this is open communication. And, 1 Timothy 5:8 warns to provide for your own household, or be the same as an unbeliever.

Would God place unrealistic expectations upon marriages and families?

We know this is not the case, and yet, He has set the bar high for good reasons. He instituted marriage as a life-long relationship and expects children born to the couple to be directed toward Him for their future relationships and eternal life.

One of the enduring aspects of marriage is how it sets up a perfect "arena" for service. As a husband and wife serve each other, they learn to focus and sacrifice for someone other than themselves. As this service grows, they become like Christ, giving themselves up for their partner as He did the church. And, this attitude of selflessness will carry through their generations as they train their children in the same manner.

A God-centered marriage goes beyond physical pleasures and companionship; it expands both husband and wife spiritually as they consider the growth of each other's walk with Jesus. A couple that loves in an earthly sense, yet has no concern for their spouse's eternity, does not exhibit the love of God.

As harsh as this may seem, God created man and woman, and united them in marriage, to be obedient to Him. This touches every detail of the body, soul, and spirit. A husband and wife should work in unison to help each other become the best biblical version of themselves.

All in all, God's expectations of marriage far exceed that of every couple, and yet, He gives us everything we need to accomplish His will.

In 2 Peter 1:3 (NIV), it says: "His divine power has given us everything we need for a godly life through our knowledge of him who called us by his own glory and goodness."

When you think of expectations, follow the path of Scripture for your marriage, and don't become weary in well-doing. Rest in God and His grace, mercy, and forbearance: He will lead you and your spouse one step at a time to flourish in your union, but He will do it His way.

Discussion Questions:

1. How do you handle unfulfilled expectations in your marriage?
2. How can you initiate a discussion on expectations with your spouse?
3. In what ways do your expectations for your marriage differ from God's?

Practical Application:

- This week, make a list of 5 realistic expectations of God that Christians can have. Discuss your list with your spouse.

Prayer:

Father God, I pray for the wisdom to see our marriage from Your perspective as a way to love my spouse as Christ loved the Church. Please help me remember that we're all imperfect souls leaning on You for wisdom. Amen.

WEEK 26: THE BLENDED FAMILY

*A new command I give you: Love one another.
As I have loved you, so you must love one
another. By this everyone will know that
you are my disciples, if you love one
another.*

— JOHN 13:34-35 NIV

The Bible is full of blended families.

The first recording of half-brothers was Isaac and Ishmael in the very first book of scripture. In the making of the nation of Israel, there was one father and four mothers. King David had a blended family, as did his son, King Solomon. None of these families were continuously operating in love, but love shines through in the moments of their greatest triumphs.

Jesus said His followers would be known for the love they have for one another. In fact, the most powerful sign of our Christian faith is love. In the above passage, Jesus is serving by washing the feet of His disciples. They were undoubtedly a blended group in which one would betray Him, and yet, He gave the example of love and servitude to all of them.

The Church is a vast blended family stretching across the globe, speaking different languages and worshipping in various methods. In the same way, our local churches mingle with multiple ethnicities, ages, and levels of spiritual maturity.

Think back to a congregational picnic or a small group pot-luck. The array of dishes is delightful to the eye and nourishing to the body and soul. The wide variety harmonizes just as it does during praise and worship, or during times of sharing and prayer.

In a blended family, harmonizing may mean extending forgiveness to your spouse and stepchildren. In some ways, they may understand each other more than you do, but with careful observation, honest communication and prayer, all can be at peace.

The building of any family takes time, and when it comes to a blended family, it may take even longer. Therefore, bring everyone together regularly for prayer, Bible study, and church attendance, so you can lay the groundwork for those bonds to form.

Something else you can do is draw other believers into your family circle for fun times and shared meals.

Sometimes, "the more, the merrier" works well, as brothers and sisters in the Lord welcome each member of your blended family without focusing on backstories, which can help blended siblings feel a stronger sense of true family unity.

Be honest with your spouse when dealing with hurt, anger, or frustration concerning their children—but keep all such conversations private. Call upon other Christian couples blessed with blended families for sharing and prayer during difficult times, and be encouraged with every bit of progress you make.

Most of all, love your blended family as God Himself would love them. Teach them His Word and help them seek His plan for their lives. When each member of a blended family understands their unique place in God's bigger family, everyone will know they belong.

Discussion Questions:

1. What are some unique skills, talents, or abilities each member brings into the family?
2. How do you think Jesus wants us to honor and love one another?
3. How can we do better as a family at praying for one another?

Practical Application:

- Make it a common practice to worship together with your children.
- Study the Bible as a group and teach Bible verses and stories.
- Practice the saying: "The family that prays together, stays together."

Prayer:

Heavenly Father of unfailing love, I pray that we are filled with a love for one another that reflects Your love for us. Thank You for blessing us with our blended family, and showing us what it's like to be part of Your heavenly family. Let us follow in Your footsteps, so our love is centered in Christ. Amen.

WEEK 27: CHERISH YOUR PARTNER

*A wife of noble character who can find? She is
worth far more than rubies.*

— PROVERBS 31:10 NIV

*Husbands, love your wives and do not be
harsh with them.*

— COLOSSIANS 3:19 NIV

What do you think of when you hear the word "cherish?"

You may have pledged to cherish your partner during your
wedding ceremony, and surely, you meant what you said.
However, as time goes by and we settle into the everyday grind

of life, we can take our spouses for granted and forget to hold them in the highest regard.

It's all too easy to overlook the most important person in our lives and even take advantage of them without meaning to, with all the stresses and strains of children, work, extended family, friends, and the like.

Ephesians 5 challenges husbands to love their wives as Christ loved the church, laying down their lives as He did, and calls for wives to respect their husbands, which is to regard and esteem them. Obedience to these commands is a daily choice, and is tested throughout the years of marriage (Crump, 2013).

Colossians 3:19 exhorts husbands to love their wives, and not to be harsh with them. Proverbs 31:10 says a wife of noble character is worth more than rubies.

We see in these passages a give and take of practice and state of being as the husband loves and gives himself up for his wife—he isn't harsh with her in word or deed. Meanwhile, the wife respects and esteems her husband, and retains a godly character that is of great worth to him.

However, as couples become familiar with each other, seeing the flaws and shortcomings of their spouse, their adherence to love, respect, giving oneself up, and functioning in godliness may sometimes fall by the wayside (Crump, 2013).

One way to keep obedience alive and well is to remember our own imperfections before our Holy God.

His unconditional love is ever ready to forgive, restore, have mercy and suffer long. Therefore, as He continues to embrace us just as we are, we carry on with patience toward our spouses —still loving, respecting, giving up the self, and growing in godliness.

Another way to forever cherish our spouse is to study their qualities. Most of us, however, are unfortunately conditioned to point out the negative aspects of our partner's character and habits, rather than focusing on the positive ones.

As you observe your husband or wife, jot down the wonderful, helpful, kind-hearted, and godly attributes they possess. Dwell on those, rather than their difficult areas, and offer them verbal praise. Here's a helpful secret: all of us strive to do and be better when our virtues are noticed and appreciated.

Cherishing one another doesn't have to stop the first time one of you falters in faith, hits a weak spot, or shows a lack of ability.

Marriages are made of two imperfect beings learning, growing, and gaining ground with the help of each other and the body of Christ. God is for you as individuals and as a couple—cherish each other as He cherishes you.

Discussion Questions:

1. Think of the ways your spouse has cherished you. What do you value most about the way they express their love (Crump, 2013)?
2. Husbands, consider the ways your wife exhibits a Godly character. What do you value most about her qualities (Crump, 2013)?

Practical Application:

- Together, create a list of 3 things your spouse does to make you feel cherished and valued in the marriage (Crump, 2013).

Prayer:

Heavenly Father, thank You for my loving spouse. Thank You for blessing me with this beautiful gift of marriage. I pray I continue to esteem my partner and show them how much love I have for them. Amen.

WEEK 28: LEADERSHIP IN LOVE AND MARRIAGE

*But I want you to realize that the head of
every man is Christ, and the head of the
woman is man, and the head of Christ
is God.*

— 1 CORINTHIANS 11:3 NIV

Is the man indeed the head of the woman?

There is much controversy surrounding this subject in today's churches. Those who oppose it see this passage to the Corinthians as outdated and sexist. Those who agree with Paul's exhortation hold the husband responsible for the family's overall functioning, especially in areas of provision and spiritual well-being.

However, the difference in roles does not indicate inequality in importance or any other aspect in the marriage. There must always be a leader, a captain, in everything: someone who steps out to oversee and to shoulder the brunt, as with any team.

Together, husbands and wives partner to make decisions, calling upon the wisdom, experience, and know-how of both parties. Each utilize their gifts, skills, and stamina to keep the family pressing on, and both answer to the truth of scripture before God.

The husband is charged with the actual leadership, much as a military officer with the responsibility and functioning of the men under his command. And, as this happens, Christ is above the man, setting the example of selfless service and love.

The spiritual leader of the house is prepared to protect, defend, and assist members of his family with their growth and relationship with God.

The husband is first in leadership. With the aid of Christ's love and Scripture, he is the final authority. However, the wife also functions as a leader, coming to him with the family's needs and offering her wisdom.

He leads as a father by bringing up the children in the training and instruction of the Lord. He teaches, commends, corrects, and leads, not by aggravating or angering, but following Christ's example of gentle guidance as his template.

As a husband, he leaves his father and mother, forsaking all others, and joins intimately to his wife.

She knows he is hers alone. He cares for her as his own body, and lives peacefully with her, so his prayers are not hindered. He lives with her in an understanding way, knowing her strengths and weaknesses, as well as what blesses her the most. He honors her as the (physically) weaker vessel—he doesn't give her more to shoulder than is tolerable throughout her seasons as a woman, wife, and mother.

These responsibilities should keep a man growing ever-closer to Christ, studying His example of servant-leadership, and improving his own way of management. His wife will look to such a partner with admiration and compassion for his weighty role in the family, and come alongside as a godly helper, to help him bear their burdens.

The man is the head of the woman, and Christ is the head of the man, and the head of Christ is God.

Discussion Questions:

1. What qualities are required of a husband who desires to fulfill his calling as spiritual leader of the home?
2. What kind of leadership did Christ display for the Church? Was it harsh or loving?
3. How can you model the characteristics of a godly husband through Christ's example?

Practical Application:

- Discuss areas in your marriage where your husband can show greater leadership. As a man, ask your partner to point out areas in which you can better lead her and the family—it may be something as simple as initiating a routine family prayer time, or planning a fun vacation for the family (Lepine, 1999).

Prayer:

Dear Heavenly Father, thank You for blessing me with the great responsibility of leading my home and family. I ask that You continue to bless me with wisdom so I may lead by Christ's example and glorify You. Amen.

WEEK 29: KEEPING THE FAMILY TOGETHER DURING TIMES APART

*For though I am absent from you in body, I
am present with you in spirit and delight
to see how disciplined you are and how
firm your faith in Christ is.*

— COLOSSIANS 2:5 NIV

Few couples picture spending extended time away from their partner when they exchange their wedding vows.

However, husbands or wives may need to make business trips, face deployments, or be called upon to assist a distant parent after a major surgery or illness. These times apart can last for varying lengths of time.

Paul said in Colossians that, although he was absent in body, he was present in spirit. It's the same with you and your spouse. This gives both of you an opportunity to "work out" your marriage, just as he told believers to "work out" their salvation in Philippians 2:12 (Prater, 2008). And, this is much easier to do, if you have a game plan.

First, have a thorough discussion with your spouse concerning the particulars of the trip, and decide the best times to communicate. If feasible, read the same Christian devotional or book of the Bible, and share from your reading at regular intervals. Openly discuss safeguards to ensure the purity of your marriage, as time spent apart can be used by the enemy to drive wedges between married couples.

Be open and honest about needs that may arise at home, but look forward to drawing closer to the Lord through mutual Bible study and prayer. When lonely, make sure both of you turn to the Lord, who will provide support, joy, comfort, and encouragement.

Keep in mind that short intervals apart can enhance the closeness in a marriage, and may even help you gain a new appreciation of your spouse's role in your union.

If children are in the household, prepare them for their parent's time away as appropriate for their ages. While apart, little ones can color pictures to send to their absent parent, or save them and make a book for them to enjoy when they return home.

They may like crossing off the days on a calendar until the family is reunited or drawing a cell phone on the day's calls are expected.

Older kids can shoulder more responsibility for younger siblings, help cook, or do additional chores. They can also enjoy taking turns leading in family devotions and prayer—which will also help prepare them to be spiritual leaders in the future.

Time apart can draw marriages and families together, strengthening bonds and deepening the team spirit, as long as God is kept first and included throughout the process.

Discussion Questions:

1. Think about a time when you and your spouse have been apart—how did God meet your needs?
2. Plan ahead: think about how you and the kids will deal with situations that you and your spouse typically handle together.
3. Use technology to help you "meet" and communicate while apart!
4. Consider Romans 8:28: ask yourselves: "what good can come from our time apart?"
5. Consider incorporating the children into daily prayer for the family, and your spouse, during times away. It will help remind them that God is the center and focus during this time, and that the family is connected through Christ, regardless of physical distance.

Practical Application:

- Separately, write down all the reservations you're having about your spouse's departure. Include scenarios that may occur and thoughts and feelings you're experiencing (Prater, 2008).
- Then, review your lists together, allowing them to serve as talking points.
- Once you're reunited with your spouse, recheck your lists to see how God met your needs (always receive your partner's list with understanding and compassion).

Prayer:

Heavenly Father, having my spouse away from home is difficult. Please help me let go of my fears and stay strong. Please fill me with Your Holy Spirit during this season, and help me feel Your comforting presence. Amen.

WEEK 30: RAISING YOUR CHILDREN
UP WITH GOD

We will not hide them from their descendants;
we will tell the next generation the
praiseworthy deeds of the Lord, his power,
and the wonders he has done.

— PSALM 78:4 NIV

Raising your children in the Lord is about leading as parents who recognize their utter dependence on the direction of the Holy Spirit, and influence of Jesus Christ. This is one of the most important responsibilities as a parent, affecting our children's eternal destinies.

The children of Israel determined to pass the praiseworthy and magnificent deeds God had performed with His almighty power to their children and grandchildren. They understood the impact of retelling their history, and the covenantal blessings of God affecting their future. Without deliberate training, their generations would lose the foundational truths of Israel's existence and God's plan for all of humankind.

When we provide our children with the same intentional instruction, and model our lives in step with God's Word, we create an atmosphere for spiritual development—especially during their formative years. Also, surrounding your children with the family of God, by routinely taking them to church, helps reinforce what's taught at home.

Ephesians 6:4 speaks directly to fathers, warning and urging them to bring up their children in the training and instruction of the Lord, and not to anger or frustrate them, which can turn them away from their efforts. Proverbs 6:20 warns children to listen and not to forsake their mother's teaching. Therefore, we see both parents are directed to instill the ways of the Lord in the household.

To deny our children spiritual nurturing deprives them of their right to learn about the One who made them, loves them, and desires to be in a relationship with them, both in this life, and throughout eternity. There can be no excuses in this area.

Teaching your children the Word of God requires your own study and understanding of His commands and teachings. When you know His precepts, you can point them out during everyday interactions with your children, using prime moments to relay the goodness of God, His plan of salvation, and guidelines for holy living.

Proverbs says whoever loves their child will discipline him; then their son will bring rest and delight. Through discipline, there is hope.

Likewise, 2 Timothy 2:15 urges us to present ourselves to God as one who is approved, not needing to be ashamed, but correctly handling the Word of Truth.

When parents know the Word, teach the Word and live the Word, their children have well-rounded examples to learn from and follow. In addition, they know their parents possess the wisdom of the Lord, and are more likely to keep their questions inside the family setting.

That said, don't exclude other mature, Christian adults such as grandparents, Sunday School teachers, and youth leaders, as they can be dependable allies in the spiritual well-being of your children. Seek their counsel as needed, and share the family circle when tough questions and prayers are required.

Bringing your children up in the fear and instruction of the Lord will be one of the most trying yet rewarding aspects of parenting; and one the Lord Himself looks upon with blessing and favor.

Discussion Questions:

1. Think about your young self and what your understanding of the Bible was when you were growing up. What do you think of your children's understanding of the Bible?

2. How are you preparing your children to know and understand the Word of God?

3. Are you taking enough time to rest and rejuvenate, so your children can see the gospel work of peace and poise in the home?

4. How can you help nurture your children's God-given passion?

Practical Application:

- Plan a prayer routine with your children. Schedule a regular time and date to pray and study the Lord's Word with your kids.

Prayer:

Father God, amidst all the distractions of the world, I pray that You give us the tools and wisdom to devote ourselves to teaching our children the works of God. We pray they receive spiritual nourishment, so they come to love You and know about Your good and marvelous deeds. Amen.

WEEK 31: SHARE YOUR WEAKNESSES WITH YOUR SPOUSE

But he said to me, "My grace is sufficient for you, for my power is made perfect in weakness." Therefore I will boast all the more gladly about my weaknesses, so that Christ's power may rest on me.

— 2 CORINTHIANS 12:9 NIV

Marriage is the union of two imperfect people with individual weaknesses relying on the strength of our perfect Lord and Savior. When viewed as the Lord sees them, our weaknesses can be a gift from God, causing us to lean more fully into Him, recognizing our needs and dependent nature.

Paul said he would boast in his weaknesses, so Christ's power could rest on him. Likewise, God can use situations in our lives to show that He is the source of our strength, power, joy and hope, as well as to show us how we must bring our weaknesses to Him, in order to partner with His power.

It's futile to stand in pride and self-reliance, believing each of us can handle our own imperfections. If that were the case, weaknesses would no longer exist. Psalm 28:7 says the Lord is our strength and our shield, and that our hearts can trust in Him and receive His help. It speaks of a joyful heart, and singing praises to the One who helps.

When difficulties arise, we can look to Him; surrendering our weaknesses and asking for His strength to come forth in tangible ways.

You may often be unaware of your weaknesses until time spent with your spouse reveals them in a new light. Rather than defend yourself, as before an opponent, you can team up with your spouse, and present your frailties to the Lord.

Sharing your struggles, praying together, and working to help each other become the best biblical version of yourselves brings Christ's power into your marriage. This shared reliance on His strength puts both husband and wife on equal footing before the throne of God—one of humility.

Therefore, humility before God and your spouse can set the stage for more profound communion—that of accepting assistance from both.

Paul didn't rejoice in his weaknesses just because he had them, nor did he enjoy them as if to make up an excuse to keep them. Instead, he rejoiced because of the dependency they caused upon him in the Lord, and the humility they brought into his life. He delighted in seeing God's power at work despite himself.

When faced with personal weaknesses, confess them before God's throne, finding grace and help in time of need. Then, lean into God and His mercy, determined to grow in His strength.

Weaknesses send us to the Lord—in that, we rejoice, knowing our Heavenly Father possesses everything we lack, and solutions to all our difficulties. In Him, we are more than conquerors.

Discussion Questions:

1. What areas of your marriage do you feel God wants you to ask Him for strength?
2. What are some ways you have seen Christ's strength manifested in your marriage when faced with a challenge?
3. What are some ways God has manifested His strength and power for you as a parent? Did you tell your children where you derived your source of power?

Practical Application:

- Read Isaiah 40:29 with your spouse.

- Then, separately, make a list of 3 weaknesses for which you need the Lord to be your source of strength.
- Finally, come together, review and discuss the list with your spouse.

Prayer:

Dear God, help me see my weaknesses as an opportunity to depend on Your power. I pray that You enable my spouse and me to rely on Your strength in every challenge we face. Amen.

WEEK 32: FORGIVENESS FROM THE HEART

For if you forgive other people when they sin against you, your heavenly Father will also forgive you. But if you do not forgive others their sins, your Father will not forgive your sins.

— MATTHEW 6:14-15 NIV

Forgiveness is a cornerstone in every relationship, and forgiving your spouse while not holding a grudge is essential to building a marriage with a solid foundation.

God's forgiveness includes no longer holding the past against us, and also seeing us through the eyes of Jesus' obedience on the cross. His actions washed our sins away! This was not an easy process, as our Lord suffered and died beneath the weight of our transgressions. And yet, it was effective. It is this same Savior who warns and instructs us to forgive, continuously.

He didn't say to forgive if we believe the other person deserves it, but from a heart of obedience to God.

Imagine if God refused to forgive, or calculated our current merit each time we needed His forgiveness. What if He showed favoritism, forgiving one of His children for a specific sin, but not another? What if His forgiveness depended on His mood, as in some pagan religions, or we had to cry out and cut ourselves before He heard our pleas for mercy?

As believers in Christ Jesus and the written Word of God, we have the perfect example of divine forgiveness, examples of unforgiveness, and the command to forgive seventy times seven when our brother sins against us. (Matthew 18:21-22). However, Jesus is not asking us here to keep score, and when your spouse sins against you for the 491st time, for example, forgiveness has run out. Instead, He's giving us a command for ongoing, long-term forgiveness, just as He forgives us.

Does this mean we allow our spouse or children to sin against us in willful disobedience to Scripture, yet forgive and forget? No, it means we forgive while holding our loved ones accountable, seeking the Lord's guidance, and the spiritual authority He's given us, as a way to handle patterns of sin.

Even when our spouse's sorrow and repentance are genuine, and our own forgiveness is just as real, sometimes the hurt, anger, and frustration of a particular sin will take time to heal. When this happens, we must cling to the Lord, to His Word, and possibly seek counsel. The end goal should be to do everything you can for the sake of restoration, as far as it concerns you.

Forgiveness is no easy task: it cost the life of our Lord and Savior. So, when you look into the eyes of your spouse, remember first your own need for forgiveness, and extend the love of God to them, as He continuously extends it to you.

Even if forgiveness comes gradually, as if layer after layer of an offense must be peeled back and dealt with bit by bit—it is still forgiveness.

Discussion Questions:

1. In which circumstances do you find it hard to accept your spouse's forgiveness?
2. Are there circumstances where you find it hard to forgive yourself?
3. Are there any old wounds that are creating distance between you and your spouse? If so, take a moment to discuss and resolve them. Does an apology need to be made, or forgiveness rendered?
4. Can you think of an example from your own life when God has forgiven you multiple times?

Practical Application:

- Read Ephesians 4:32 (NIV): "Be kind and compassionate to one another, forgiving each other just as in Christ God forgave you." Talk to your partner about a time you were hurt, and how God helped you to forgive.

Prayer:

Heavenly Father, thank You for forgiving me over and over, even when I don't deserve it. I ask that You give me the grace to forgive my spouse just as You have forgiven me. Amen.

WEEK 33: PUTTING PRIDE ASIDE

God opposes the proud but shows favor to the humble.

— JAMES 4:6 NIV

A strong marriage begins with humility, while pride that is rooted in selfishness and arrogance can cause the relationship to crumble.

Many conflicts between husband and wife spring from a prideful, closed heart, demanding its way, from a core belief of superiority. Only when humility has done its work can a marriage thrive without the injury of pride.

God shows favor or grace to the humble. These words are recorded three times in scripture: in James 4:6, Proverbs 3:34, and 1 Peter 5:5.

They are foundational to our understanding of our personal relationship with God, and that, while we all desire His favor, it doesn't come automatically—it requires the prerequisite of humility.

Within marriage, the call to humility is an assault on our selfish pride.

We all have it, but sometimes it's hidden.

Suppose, for example, you successfully complete a significant project at work and earn praise as the best in your department. You enjoy the applause and put even greater effort into your next project, while enjoying the ongoing accolades. Then, without conscious thought, you take your air of superiority home to your spouse.

The fact is, whether it is others or our own inner conversations which bolster our fleshly pride; pride is something that lurks in the depths of our character, always waiting for the right opportunity to present itself.

Has your spouse ever pricked your pride? And, rather than viewing a particular interaction as an opportunity to grow in humility, did you react as if their statement or request were a direct hit to your ego?

Ephesians 5:26 speaks of husbands cleansing their wives with the washing of water through the Word. How painful such a "washing" could be if it's seen as a direct attack, rather than gentle instruction.

Matthew 20:28 teaches that Jesus came into the world not to be served, but to serve. Can you graciously follow His lead without the kind of acknowledgments you may receive at work?

Marriage is a spiritual opportunity: if we use it to learn how to walk in the footsteps of Jesus, serving our spouses and families with all humility of heart, mind, and hand.

As you look to the interests of your husband or wife, diligently honoring their needs and wishes with an attitude of selflessness, your children will gain insight into the walk of the Spirit. Furthermore, your legacy of servitude will even pass to future generations.

However, if your children witness power struggles, complaints about offering assistance, or negligence concerning obvious needs, they'll learn to put themselves first—not only in their own families, but throughout the various areas of life.

Pride refuses to listen, lend a hand, or discuss with words and tones conducive to mutual edification.

Instead, it says, "me first, my way, and in my time."

Imagine the Lord Jesus with such an attitude or mode of functioning. He would have never accomplished the work of our salvation, never set an example for our lives on this earth, or cared to receive us into His glory.

Do yourself and your loved ones a big favor: put pride aside!

Discussion Questions:

1. How does pride destroy marriages?
2. What are some signs of pride in your marriage? Is this something that your children may pick up?

Practical Application:

- Together, read Philippians 2:4 (NIV): "Not looking to your own interests but each of you to the interests of others."
- Use this passage as a point of discussion. If pride creates opposition in marriage, humility renders grace. How does grace bring you and your spouse closer to one another?

Prayer:

Heavenly Father, I pray that You help me let go of pride, giving me the courage to humble myself like Jesus, so I may serve my spouse in a Christ-like manner. Amen.

WEEK 34: GOD-GIVEN PARTNERSHIP IN PARENTING

Two are better than one, because they have a
good return for their labor.

— ECCLESIASTES 4:9 NIV

The secular formula for relationships says opposites attract.

Therefore, if we were to follow this saying, an extrovert connects with an introvert, and one with dry humor combines well with one who has wit and charm. However, blessed are the children of God who mesh together not as polar opposites, but with interlocking gifts and callings that build individual families and the family of God.

In 1 Corinthians 12, we learn that we've been given a variety of gifts, but all from the same Spirit—and different kinds of service, but from the same Lord. These are provided for the common good: some receive messages of wisdom or knowledge, some a greater measure of faith, etc.

Romans 12 lists prophecy, ministering, teaching, exhortation, giving, leading, mercy and serving as some of the gifts God gives to people.

Imagine the spiritual possibilities when you view your marriage as a union of gifts, rather than opposites. You may possess gifts of giving and teaching, while your spouse functions in serving and faith—complimenting each other spiritually, rather than opposing one another.

Your children can benefit from the meshing of your God-given gifts too, as you make decisions, discipline, and direct each of them. In times of conflict, one parent may lead with more assertive discipline, while the other reassures with mercy.

When decisions are made, one parent may exude more faith than the other or have unique wisdom concerning a subject. When planning, one parent may be pleased to research and examine the budget, while the other is ready to carry out the plan as a cheerful servant—again, working as a team for the goodness of the family unit.

When the Spirit of God instilled gifts into each of His children, none of these were meant to be used for self-gratification, but to build up, perfect and serve the body of Christ. The same principle works within marriage and family: your God-given gifts are there to build, never to compete or defeat, but to complement.

To grow and mature in the use of your gifts, you must, of course, know them first! You may have already discerned them from those among the lists recorded in Scripture, or from the type of work and ministries you find invigorating and fulfilling. Your spouse and spiritually-minded friends can also recognize your God-given gifts, and help you see them, if you ask them.

Some partners, fully accepting each other's gifts, know who does what in the marriage, as well as in parenting. This goes beyond splitting household chores, or deciding who bathes the baby: it's more about who's more inclined to pray first, who already knows the scriptural instructions on a topic, or maybe who has the best delivery for discipline, and who gives from the heart when a reward is in order.

However, as you lean on and glean from your partner's spiritual gifts, be sure to focus on developing your own as well, studying how they blend together to help raise and bless your children. When you believe that your children are also a gift, you will desire to be an example for them, and show them that mom and dad are something better than opposites—mom and dad are a spiritual *team*.

Discussion Questions:

1. How do your spouse's character traits encourage the children in the home?
2. Discuss the different ways your partner approaches conflict in the home.
3. What spiritual gifts do you want your children to learn from your relationship with God and your spouse?

Practical Application:

- Make a list of the ways your spouse's personal and spiritual gifts contribute to the household, and share them with each other (Hawley, 2018).

Prayer:

Dear Lord, thank You for bringing my spouse and me together as one, and for all their spiritual and personal gifts. I pray that You continue to help us grow in our union so we may nurture our children's gifts. Amen.

WEEK 35: ACCEPTING HELP

Carry each other's burdens, and in this way
you will fulfill the law of Christ.

— GALATIANS 6:2 NIV

Chances are, you're an expert at carrying the burdens of others.

You've probably cooked meals, dropped off groceries, babysat, went shopping, fixed cars, and picked things up for church. And, even more, you've probably sought the Lord on your knees for brothers and sisters in Christ.

Now, how often would you allow someone else to do these very things for you?

At times, we refuse such help due to pride.

For example, we may feel terrible physically, but the house is a mess, so we wouldn't dare let anyone drop off a meal. Or maybe we're experiencing grief or hurt, and could really benefit from some on-the-spot prayer, but won't share our emotional upsets with others for fear they may be seen as weaknesses.

Think of a young couple that could use a break.

They've been working long hours, and their little one has kept them up at night. Their older kids need rides to after-school activities, and their extended family has called upon them a few times in the past week. Perhaps taking a few hours away from the house would infuse them with the renewed strength they so desperately need. Instead, however, they're embarrassed by their children's behavior and won't ask anyone to watch them.

It can be humbling to admit we need help, but letting others come alongside to assist us can open doors for deeper fellowship, and allows others to use their spiritual gifts as God intended. Sometimes, our closest friends are found through acts of service, and God is pleased to see His children reaching out to each other from within His family.

How often do you present your needs to your spouse? In marriage, there should be no secret struggles. When you carry each other's burdens, you're strengthening the couple's unity and deepening your bonds. This fulfills the law of Christ, who said to love our neighbors as unto ourselves.

Sometimes a couple fails to recognize that their spouse is their neighbor too, as well as their brother or sister in the Lord. They apply scriptures that directly concern marriage only, and in doing so, deprive each other of the full benefits of fellowship within the marriage.

But here's a secret: when we accept help from our spouses, we permit them to receive support from us as well! And, as serving one another becomes a natural part of teamwork, it sets a Christ-like example to any children in the home, (who you can be sure, are always watching and learning from our actions).

But don't limit help to things accomplished with a strong back, or willing hands: asking for help includes sharing prayer requests and letting your spouse know whenever you need a listening ear, or help to brainstorm a solution to a problem at work or in ministry.

Think of all the ways you're willing to assist others, including your spouse, and determine to overcome your personal objections to letting others do the same for you. If pride prevents you from asking for help, ask the Lord to help you become a humble and gracious receiver—you will be surprised with the results.

Discussion Questions:

1. Think about a time when you declined help from others. What stopped you from allowing them to serve you?

2. When your spouse offers to help you, do you often ignore it?

3. How can you be more open to allowing your spouse to love you through acts of service?

Practical Application:

- Together with your spouse, read Hebrews 4:16 (NIV): "Let us then approach God's throne of grace with confidence, so that we may receive mercy and find grace to help us in our time of need."

- Discuss the passage. Then, make a list of all those people that God has placed in your lives to help you.

Prayer:

Father God, I pray for the wisdom to know when I need help, and the humility to accept it when someone offers. Amen.

WEEK 36: TEACHING OUR KIDS TO HONOR THEIR PARENTS

Honor your father and your mother, so that
you may live long in the land the Lord
your God is giving you.

— EXODUS 20:12 NIV

We all desire to live under God's blessing, and He tells us how to do that in very simple terms: one way is simply to honor our parents. Think about your relationship with your parents as you were growing up: did you honor them as a way of life, or walk in obedience to God's command to honor?

You may recognize that your honor to your parents, or lack thereof, was also reflected in your attitude toward other authority figures, and ultimately, your walk with God. And, no doubt, you desire for your children to understand the dynamics of honor, which will also affect crucial areas of their lives.

When you teach your children to honor you, you're honoring God with your obedience, while teaching them to fear the Lord. Children who learn to honor their parents will indeed be blessed throughout their lives.

However, consider a child that has disregarded their parents from a young age—they don't obey, they talk back, speak ill of their parents, and go behind their backs, breaking family rules. Such a child is sinning against the Fifth Commandment, and forfeiting God's blessing promised to those who honor their parents.

Proverbs 30:17 says the eye that mocks a father or scorns an aging mother will be pecked out by the ravens of the valley and eaten by vultures. This is figurative, but it denotes severe punishment.

Ephesians 6:1 tells children to obey their parents in the Lord, because it's the right thing to do. Obedience is not a recommendation, but a command, passing blessing or discipline down through the generations, depending on a child's adherence to it.

These scriptures do not assume obedience to parents as something that's always easy, however. Children will not always agree with their parents, but they're still called to obey just the same. Jesus certainly knew more than his earthly parents, and yet, He obeyed them and gave honor and care to His mother, even when dying on the cross. Furthermore, His very death was in direct obedience to the will of His Heavenly Father.

Respect for parents is the foundation of a moral and good society.

When children listen to their parents' words, they'll be more likely to listen to the instructions of the Lord throughout their lives, and thus receive the blessings of obedience.

Discussion Questions:

1. Do you believe your children treat you with honor and respect?
2. What are some ways God has called you to honor your parents or other elders around you?
3. What is the connection between honoring God and honoring your parents?
4. What kind of example have you set for your kids when it comes to honoring your parents?

Practical Application:

- Ask your older children to look up Bible stories about honoring fathers. Select one Bible verse and discuss different ways the children in it honored their father (Kummer, 2011). (If your children are young, read a verse with your spouse and reflect on ways you can honor our Father in Heaven.) Here are some good examples you can use:

- Luke 15:11-32: "The Parable of the Prodigal Son."
- Genesis 47:1-11: "Joseph provides for his aged father."
- Genesis 22:1-19: "Abraham almost sacrifices Isaac."

Prayer:

Dear Lord, You are the author of parenting. Please show us how we can honor our parents by honoring You, and thus receive your blessings of obedience. Help our children honor other elders, and us, so they too can obtain Your favor and enjoy a long and blessed life. Amen.

WEEK 37: INVESTING IN YOUR PERSONAL GROWTH

*... and the two will become one flesh. So they
are no longer two, but one flesh.*

— MARK 10:8 NIV

And so, the two become one flesh and are no longer two.

Does this mean Christian couples forgo their personal identities and become lost in the oneness of marriage? Do they give up all individual hopes, dreams, and desires? Are their goals dissolved as if no longer worthy or essential?

If the answer to any of these questions were to be "yes," very few would marry!

If this were truly to be the case, then what would even be the point in planning? If both his and her dreams, goals, and desires were to no longer be valid, what would the determining factors be when creating a third, or neutral, plan for the both of them?

Marriage should help develop, not cancel, both partner's individuality.

Think of the beauty of having your partner's aid in becoming all you can be. Such support can only come from the most intimate person in your life. As such, while you labor together to ensure the success of both, the bond of oneness is achieved.

In 1 Corinthians 12:12-31, Paul speaks of the body of Christ as a fellowship of many individuals using their God-given gifts to perfect the functioning of the whole. If members were no longer distinct in their gifts and calling, it would hinder the work of the Lord.

Remember that hopes, dreams, and goals develop and grow when planted in the most fertile soil. When you provide a sounding board for your partner's ideas, you not only communicate your love to them, but also your regard for them as a person.

The oneness of marriage says, "I am for you," and "I will back you." It searches, assists and stretches as needed to help each person become the best biblical version of themselves.

Be honest with your spouse about your goals and desires for personal growth. Together, construct a plan that will accomplish them bit by bit. Your goals can be physical, spiritual, educational, career-minded, or relational. Some will cost money, while others will cost time and energy; and your spouse may need to fill in the temporary gaps while you settle into the new processes.

However, as you take turns with extra allowance and assistance, your appreciation and admiration for each other will deepen. You will find new ways for the two of you to become one at home: in the extended family, in worship, and sometimes even in the field of work.

When couples remain focused on God's image within their spouse, and recognize the gifts, talents, and skills He has infused within them, they can join in on the exciting adventure of becoming one while remaining two.

And, as we read at the start of this devotional, two enjoy a greater return for their work!

Discussion Questions:

1. What are your most desired dreams and goals? What steps can you take to bring them to fruition? Does your spouse support your goals and dreams?
2. Do you both agree to the idea of taking time out of your schedule to nurture your goals/desires?
3. Is lifelong education important to you? (Be it formal or informal)

4. Do you support your spouse in their desire to pursue personal and spiritual development?

Practical Application:

- Make a list of your top 3 goals/dreams, then come together and share them with your spouse.

Prayer:

Dear Heavenly Father, thank You for creating me as I am. I ask that You continue to develop me as an individual, so that I can function as one alongside my spouse in this marriage. Amen.

WEEK 38: INVESTING TIME IN YOUR MARRIAGE (WITHOUT THE KIDS)

That is why a man leaves his father and
mother and is united to his wife, and they
become one flesh.

— GENESIS 2:24 NIV

When you fell in love with your partner, it was just the two of you. You looked forward to every phone call and date night, and dreamed of the day you'd pledge your lives to each other.

After you said, "I do," it was still just you two, and you found something to enjoy together at the end of the day, and made plans for your weekends, and no one (hopefully) interfered. You smiled through candlelit dinners, held hands in the park, snuggled up for movie night, cooked in the kitchen, read together, prayed together, argued together, and then made up! Everything you did was together.

Now, when the children come, you're still together, sure, but in a way that is now challenged by the learning curve and demands of parenting. Now, instead of reading your favorite devotional together, you're researching newborn sleep patterns, when to introduce solid foods, and surfing the web comparing reviews of the safest strollers and high chairs to purchase.

The beauty of parenting is in sharing a little creation of God; a magnificent blessing that blends you and your spouse in a new, intimate and joyful way. And the same happens with each new child—you are, once again, overcome with the incredible work of the Lord in unison with your partner.

However, if you're not careful in this process, it can be very easy to lose your way.

Becoming a parent, while losing sight of being a husband or wife, might make you an expert mom or dad, sure, but can also set you back in unity and closeness within your marriage.

The Bible speaks of the act of "cleaving." In the Old Testament, cleaving meant to cling to, or stick to. In the New Testament, it means to glue together, or upon. Either way, the reference points to a tight, inseparable bond (Crump, 2013).

If a man is to leave his father and mother and cleave, cling, stick, or be glued to his wife, where do we figure in the children?

Their parents, (that's you and your spouse), are meant to be "stuck together like glue upon glue." Although children most definitely need the attention, care, nurturing, teaching, and leadership of their parents, these things are best accomplished as a tasteful "side-dish" to the main course of marriage.

Bottom line: Don't allow parenting, or anything else, create distance in your relationship with your spouse, as this will also inevitably affect your ability to be a good parent too, in the long run.

In every aspect, children are something you do together, then turn to each other for intentional time alone. Remember that you were united with your partner before the children came along, and marriage is for life—direct parenting is only until each child leaves the home.

Remember those date nights, walks in the park, movies and popcorn? The laughter in the middle of the night? They may take more planning once you become parents, but the two are still one, and within that sacred union, children are additions, not replacements.

Discussion Questions:

1. Read 1 Corinthians 3:10-15. Reflect on the principles from this passage: what do you think God wants you to understand and apply here (Crump, 2013)?
2. How can you be sure you're building your marriage

with a foundation of gold, silver, and costly stones (Crump, 2013)?

3. What does quality time look like in your marriage?

Practical Application:

- Participate in an activity you can do with your spouse this week that can help you strengthen the glue that holds the two of you together.

Prayer:

Father God, thank You for the bond between my spouse and me. I pray that we continue to strengthen our relationship by prioritizing and spending quality time with one another. Amen.

WEEK 39: YOU ARE NOT ALONE; GOD IS WITH YOU

Have I not commanded you? Be strong and courageous. Do not be afraid; do not be discouraged, for the Lord your God will be with you wherever you go.

— JOSHUA 1:9 NIV

Before we arrive at Joshua 1:9, the Lord had already told Joshua to be strong and courageous twice before.

This third time, God asks the rhetorical question: "Have I not commanded you?" He was referencing the time Joshua was named Moses' successor in Deuteronomy 31:6-7. In this third instance, the Lord reminded Joshua not only of what he must do, but also of what he must not be: frightened or dismayed (Michael, 2018).

Really, think about this command.

Could Joshua, by his own will, be strong, courageous, and fearless? Either he was, or he wasn't. How could God command Joshua, or any of us, to be something we're not (Michael, 2018)?

The Lord is not unjust. He's not an "overlord" bearing down on His subjects with impossible rules, regulations and commands, which guarantee failure. Those are character traits He attributed to Pharaoh and other unrighteous tyrants in Scripture.

God didn't demand courage and strength from Joshua, then walk away and leave him in the struggle. He reminded him of His continuous presence, no matter where Joshua found himself.

And, this isn't the only place in the Bible where God promises His help and presence: in Hebrews 13:5, He says He will never leave us nor forsake us.

Do you draw upon His presence when you find yourself lonely in your marriage?

Remember, no marriage and no partner; in fact, no relationship of any kind, can meet your every need. Your spouse cannot fill gaps or voids meant to be filled only by the presence of God. Likewise, neither can *you* fill them for your husband or wife.

There are times when your spouse may be away on business, or busy with other temporary matters that demand greater amounts of time and attention. However, you can learn to turn these potentially lonely times into times of greater intimacy with God, use them for catching up with friends and family, re-engaging a hobby, or enjoying a good book.

On many occasions, Jesus sought solitary places for prayer. This wasn't because He was lonely, but to use the time away from his disciples to commune with the Father, which seemed to be His main activity when seeking greater closeness with God.

Consider the spiritual, and perhaps even physical rejuvenation that can happen during short seasons of loneliness within your marriage. Communicate openly about your ability to handle busy times away from each other, whether you're both in the house or temporarily away.

Whenever you have to spend some time alone, be sure to make the most of it in self-care and love, so you can then present "the refreshed you" to your partner with joy and gladness.

Discussion Questions:

1. How has God helped you turn lonely moments into positive ones?
2. Does trusting God in our times alone imply action on our part?
3. How can you create a closer connection with your spouse? For example, if your partner usually makes dinner, can you offer to help them in the kitchen?

Practical Application:

- Spend time alone and examine what you expect from your partner. Are they aware of your desires and expectations? Remember that, over time, we all grow and change. Perhaps your needs have changed too. Discuss this with your partner—don't assume they know things you haven't shared with them.

Prayer:

Heavenly Father, I know Your will in my marriage is to draw me closer to my spouse so that I won't feel alone. Please help me seek You in my times of solitude, because I know You are always with me. Amen.

WEEK 40: PARENTING WITHOUT FEAR

For the Spirit God gave us does not make us timid, but gives us power, love and self-discipline.

— 2 TIMOTHY 1:7 NIV

It's not uncommon for children to choose one parent over the other. And, just so you know, that can change at any time!

Sometimes, children prefer the parent they see as softer and more comforting, or the one that will rough-house with them, or be most willing to help them with homework.

The different ages and stages of a child's development may also direct them to one parent: usually the one they deem most able to diminish their insecurities. However, a child may not know how to articulate: "I want to be with daddy because he makes thunderstorms go away," or, "mom has more patience when teaching me to drive."

And they definitely don't equate these preferences with love for one, but not for the other. Instead, they love both, but have decided in their young minds who is better at what, and sometimes, who is even most like themselves.

However, parents shouldn't feel rejection or fear when a child prefers the opposite parent, and there's no need to be timid about parenting. The best course of action is to carry on, as usual, being the godly, growing parent you would be in any other circumstance.

Some parenting modes leave girls in the kitchen with mom and the boys out in the garage with dad. They believe girls are always better in language arts and boys in math. And some discriminate by age: the baby should never go out with dad, and a teenager has to speak with both parents whenever asking for permission to go out with friends.

In reality, the roles you and your spouse play in the lives of each of your children is whatever you agree upon: whatever works, and shows the love and acceptance of Christ. There's no need for fearful parenting, especially to win the favor of a child back from your spouse. Everything has its place and time, and also its natural part in the transition of growth.

Think of the love of God, shown so uniquely to each of His children.

Remain steadfast in your position with Him and with your children. Walk in confidence and self-control when it may be easier to feel slighted or jealous. Fearless parenting means accepting your children's preferential seasons, while being sure of who you are in Christ, and as their parent.

As your children grow and mature, they'll lean back and forth on both their parents, sometimes even when you least expect it! Keep your love steady no matter what, so they'll learn about the unconditional love of their Heavenly Father and come to respect your patience.

Do you feel uncertain about your child's attachment to you, and therefore shy away from power-filled parenting? Give your fears to God and enjoy the journey, whether it's your turn to be number one, or that of your spouse.

Discussion Questions:

1. How would you feel if your child preferred your spouse over you?
2. What can you do to keep yourself from becoming jealous or insecure during such a season?

Practical Application:

- Read John 14:27 (NIV): "Peace I leave with you; my peace I give you. I do not give to you as the world gives. Do not let your hearts be troubled and do not be afraid".
- What does this verse tell you about Christ's ability to quiet your fears and insecurities?

Prayer:

Heavenly Father, thank You for giving us our precious children. Please give us the wisdom to parent each one with Your love, and never from fear, even as the seasons change throughout their development. Amen.

WEEK 41: CALMING QUARRELS WHEN THE KIDS MAY BE WATCHING

What causes fights and quarrels among you?
Don't they come from your desires that
battle within you? You desire but do not
have, so you kill. You covet but you cannot
get what you want, so you quarrel and fight.
You do not have because you do not ask God.
When you ask, you do not receive, because
you ask with wrong motives, that you may
spend what you get on your pleasures.

— JAMES 4:1-3 NIV

Disagreements are a natural part of marriage because no two people will see things 100% the same way all the time. And sadly, some of these disagreements will inevitably happen in front of the children. However, if we take a God-centered approach to resolving the issues at hand, we can set a good example for our kids in terms of conflict resolution.

The root cause of conflict is the inherent selfishness present in all of us.

We all want to be heard, and for things to go our way from an early age, don't we? Think of a couple of two or three-year-olds. They know what they want, and think they can bully the other to get it. When that doesn't happen, they raise a fuss that's heard throughout the house!

Sometimes, arguing parents can resemble the scrimmage between two children... but what motivates their disagreements? The word "motive" comes from the Greek meaning of brokenness and sickness. This brokenness and sickness, which we all carry to one degree or another, causes us to lash out to protect ourselves and our way of thinking. We're so sure we're right because we need to remain secure.

James 4:1-5 speaks of quarreling, then comments on the sinfulness of becoming friends with the world. Arguments concerning material objects that are coveted and selfishly desired spring from such a "friendship" with the material.

When your children witness disagreements between you and their other parent, they can either learn to consult Scripture and keep the peace, or to tower over each other with raised voices and ugly words.

Romans 12:18 instructs us to live at peace with everyone, as far as it concerns us. This doesn't mean peace at *any* cost, which solves nothing, but peacefully living and working together to make God-centered decisions for the good of all.

Discussion Questions:

1. We're naturally inclined to try to win arguments. Instead of focusing on winning, think about how you can bring out the best in your spouse during the argument. Exchange ideas to help each other better handle conflict (Crump, 2013).
2. Think of the last time you disagreed in front of the kids: did you handle the conflict according to the Word of God? After reading today's scripture, how could you have taken a more God-like approach to resolve the conflict?
3. Identify controversial issues in your marriage, and think of a resolution by agreeing to honor a biblical principle (Crump, 2013).
4. Have you ever had a conflict that uncovered deeper intimacy and a greater understanding? If so, what was the outcome (Focus on the Family, 2016)?

Practical Application:

- Together, read Ephesians 4:26-32. Think back to a time when you went to bed with unresolved conflict. How did you wake up feeling the following morning? Agree with your spouse to extend any needed forgiveness before bedtime, even if you must resolve the issue in the upcoming days (Crump, 2013).

Prayer:

Father God, thank You for creating me and my spouse so uniquely. At times, we do not see eye to eye, which may cause conflict, but I pray that You provide spiritual unity in our parenting and marriage. Please guide us in the best ways to respond to each other, as we work together as an example for our children and Your glory. Amen.

WEEK 42: APPRECIATING YOUR SPOUSE

I always thank my God for you because of his grace given you in Christ Jesus.

— 1 CORINTHIANS 1:4 NIV

It's important to directly tell your spouse precisely how much you appreciate them, and why. This should involve thanking God for them in prayer, in their presence, as they bless your life in so many ways.

Gratitude is a fundamental fabric of any good relationship.

And yet, it may become easy to under-appreciate and take your partner for granted after you've been married for many years. For example: if you're asked to list the things your spouse does not do right, you may quickly jot down several items. However, if asked to name the many things they do to bless you and your children on a daily basis, you may be surprised to realize you've forgotten to take these into account.

God designed marriage as a loving covenant between two people who vow to love, support, and help one another. Therefore, your marital relationship can mirror your relationship with God. Do you recognize God's goodness to you and your family? Can you count your blessings, or do you get bogged down easily with things you wish would pass?

If you're having trouble seeing things to appreciate in your spouse, check to see if you're spending time in gratitude to God. Ask Him to open your eyes to the everyday things your spouse provides, and all the extras that bring joy to your life. When you stop to consider the gifts, skills, talents, and diligence of your spouse, not to mention their faithfulness and love, you'll find many reasons to praise and appreciate your partner and the Lord.

Conversely, if you focus much of your time on what your spouse does or does not do in negative ways, you could easily break down the union in your marriage and open the doors to deep wounding.

When thinking of ways to show your appreciation, consider words and actions that particularly bless your spouse. Sometimes, a written note left on a pillow will bring a smile and warm the heart. Other times, it's an unexpected hug that holds on a bit longer than expected, or praising them in front of others.

When appreciating your spouse, feel free to get creative! You can't always cook their favorite dinner or plan for a day away from the house, but kind and affirming words are always easy to utter, and close at hand. Use Scripture to express your thanks, or help the children draw pictures illustrating family gratitude for a parent, then make them into cards.

You can even play a game around the dinner table that teaches each family member to express gratitude.

Start with mom or dad, so the younger ones will get the idea. Each person then names something they're grateful for about every person around the table. Then, the next person does the same. Accept every attempt, and help little ones think of things they appreciate. Finally, when all have taken their turn, take a few moments to thank the Lord for making you a family.

Discussion Questions:

1. What are some ways your spouse makes you feel appreciated?
2. Name two things your spouse can do to make you feel more appreciated.
3. What are some things your spouse does for you and the family for which you are grateful?

Practical Application:

- Select one thing you can do to make your spouse feel more appreciated, and do it at least three times this week!

Prayer:

Lord Jesus, help me appreciate and value my spouse even when I myself feel underappreciated. Please remind me that I am blessed to have a godly life partner on my journey, and to be thankful. Amen.

WEEK 43: EMPATHIZING WITH YOUR SPOUSE

For we do not have a high priest who is unable
to empathize with our weaknesses, but we
have one who has been tempted in every
way, just as we are—yet he did not sin.

— HEBREWS 4:15 NIV

Empathy is the ability to understand and feel the emotions of another person.

In marriage, this means showing compassion for what your spouse has experienced in the past, and what they face in the present. Although we cannot wholly understand everything that can concern our spouse, or vice versa, there is One who can.

Hebrews tells us that Jesus, our High Priest, can empathize with our weaknesses, and has been tempted in every way—without sinning.

Consider a deep pain in your heart that seems no person can touch.

You feel alone in your sorrow or frustration and long for the fellowship of empathy. This is a time to take your thoughts and feelings to your spouse and to the Lord—the One who always meets us with mercy and grace.

"He was despised and rejected by mankind, a man of suffering, and familiar with pain. Like one from whom people hide their faces he was despised, and we held him in low esteem. Surely he took up our pain and bore our suffering, yet we considered him punished by God, stricken by him, and afflicted." (Isaiah 53:3-4,7 NIV)

Can anyone be more misunderstood, mistreated, and left utterly alone while sacrificing His very life for all those that scorned Him?

Galatians 6:2 instructs us to bear each other's burdens to fulfill the law of Christ, yet it's much easier, and much more enjoyable, to be with someone who's full of joy and a good time.

Empathy calls upon you to exercise active listening, and emotionally switch places with your spouse, to better understand their position. It's a privilege to listen and carry their troubles as if they were your own, and it communicates your desire to see your partner comforted and at peace.

When we empathize in our marriage, we're telling the other person that they have value and are worth our time and attention. When we fail to listen, or dismiss their pain, we communicate non-importance, or even disdain.

Want to become more empathetic with your spouse?

Learn to listen without judgment. Lean close, giving them your undivided attention, and offer a gesture of care and concern. You may not be able to solve their problem or take away their sorrow, but you can snuggle silently, listen long, and ask our all-knowing Lord to touch their hearts with His comfort. Such acts alone can make all the difference. And, more often than not, could even be all that's necessary.

Discussion Questions:

1. How can you empathize with your spouse when they're going through a difficult time? For example, how can a spouse show empathy for their partner when they get up to feed the baby in the middle of the night?
2. In what ways can empathy help us love our neighbors as we love ourselves?
3. Read Matthew 7:12: in what ways can our ability to be empathic help us apply this verse in our lives?

Practical Application:

- Together, read 1 Corinthians 12:26 (NIV): "If one part suffers, every part suffers with it; if one part is honored, every part rejoices with it." Use this as a talking point with your spouse. What does this verse tell us about empathizing with others?

Prayer:

Father God, please help us show empathy in our marriage. Please help us listen actively, and respond in grace. Lord God, Your Son is empathetic because He has endured His own trials and tribulations, so we may have life. Please help us be more like Him. We pray this in His precious and holy name. Amen.

WEEK 44: CONSTANT COMMUNICATION AMIDST ALL OF LIFE'S CHANGES

*I have told you these things, so that in me you
may have peace. In this world you will
have trouble. But take heart! I have
overcome the world.*

— JOHN 16:33 NIV

Every marriage faces change, stress and crisis.

Whether it's a global pandemic that calls for a drastic change in how your family operates, a major move, or obtaining a more demanding career—coping well requires accepting the challenges, while increasing our trust in the Lord.

How can we accept such upheaval as part of God's plan, and rest assured that He'll see us through each time?

First, we read in the above passage that earthly troubles are inevitable.

Jesus touched on this fact in what is called His "Farewell Discourse" to His disciples. They wouldn't have lives of ease and comfort, and He warned them of such. So, as we can see here, God is well-aware of the inevitability of troubles in life, and He's already ahead on your path, standing ready to assist as challenges arise.

Second, we're promised that, in Jesus, we can have peace. This is a peace that surpasses all understanding and comes from Him alone. Of course, we can look to others for support, and discuss solutions with our spouses, but the internal and unexplainable peace that we all truly need comes only from the Lord.

Lastly, we're called to create a biblical plan of attack.

This is achieved as you and your spouse discuss the change or obstacle in detail, search the Scriptures together for guidance and pray for step-by-step direction. This also requires frequent check-ins to assess your progress, and to support one another emotionally.

One mistake couples make is acknowledging a difficulty, going to prayer, then walking away into the storm without reconvening to see what's working and what's not working as they make their way through it. This can lead to disagreements and added stress. When tensions fly, stop and reevaluate—something you're doing (or not doing) may need adjustment.

In John 16:32, Jesus spoke to His disciples about His impending death and their upcoming desertion, yet still comforted them, noting that there is peace in Him. It's important to note the full, open, and difficult conversations the Lord broached with His followers. He didn't lull them to sleep with illusions of beauty and bliss—instead, He was frank, and desired for them to stay alert.

This same attitude of wakeful watching is necessary for your marriage and family. And hear me out here—it's not that we're going to go on a morbid search for problems, but acknowledge that they will arise, so we do not become surprised and are caught off guard when they do.

When you and your spouse face issues inside or outside of your marriage, come forward and talk things out, including the Word, uniting in prayer, and relying on the peace of God.

He has given you His promise that you are not alone.

Discussion Questions:

1. As a couple, how do you expect the different stages of life to affect your marriage? (Childbirth, parenting, physical separations, financial setbacks, empty nest, illness, aging.) (Focus on the Family, 2016)
2. Do you have a community of friends or family that can provide a reliable support system when necessary?
3. Think about some challenges you've already endured

in your marriage: how did God shape these experiences
to become opportunities for learning and growth?

Practical Application:

- Together, read James 1:2-4: how has your faith been
  tested in your personal life and marriage? Can you
  recognize greater patience in yourself and your spouse
  due to such testing?

Prayer:

Dear Heavenly Father, please help us conquer the various stages
of life together. Help us lean on You and each other, and be an
example to other couples in our circle of friends and family.
Amen.

WEEK 45: THE NEVER-ENDING TO-DO LIST (IT'S OKAY NOT TO GET EVERYTHING DONE!)

From the ends of the earth I call to you, I call as my heart grows faint; lead me to the rock that is higher than I.

— PSALM 61:2 NIV

Throughout your married life, there will be nights when you fall into bed feeling overwhelmed with responsibilities, and mornings where you arise with the same demanding thoughts racing through your mind. As a result of caring for your family, work, school, finances and other commitments, you may find yourself feeling overextended, under-rested, and under-prayed.

During these seasons, you may also face burn-out and undue stress, leaving little time to nurture yourself and your marriage.

However, there is relief when you turn to Jesus for guidance and perspective.

Consider a woman who's been at home for seven months with her first child. She struggles with feelings of inadequacy as she looks around at a once-neat and tidy home. Or, imagine a parent that is working from home while also attempting to homeschool during a pandemic. Or, maybe, a couple who welcomes a parent into their home when least expected.

All of these examples reflect the average homelife of an American family. Most wish to simplify their lives, but don't know how to achieve it. When they sit down to figure it out, things get so complicated they don't even know where to start.

How did we get to a place of such break-neck activity and mile-long "to-do" lists? Usually, this happens when we take our eyes off our legitimate priorities to "scan the horizon" of what else might be out there. In other words, when we start focusing too much on the future, and not enough on the present. This results in unnecessary clutter, both in schedule and material possessions, which inevitably ends up crowding out the essentials.

Think about your lists as they stand right now: who are the people for which you're responsible? How should you be serving them? What generates even more energy when you put effort into it?

Ask the Lord to reveal misplaced priorities that are adding undue burdens, then refocus on His lists for your lives, specifically those found in Scripture. Finally, call out to Him, and invite Him to those areas that are needing some genuine attention, waiting on Him to direct and order all things, as only He can and knows how. It is never His will that you make a business of busyness, but that you take the time to rest in Him and rely on His strength.

Are there items on your "to-do" list that can be checked off due to lack of importance, or left for days with more energy? Be realistic, and let them go as necessary. This will open you up to the things that actually matter most, and also to receiving the refreshment and rest that you actually need!

Discussion Questions:

1. What's one thing you can do to trust God when you're overwhelmed?
2. How can you help your partner when they're feeling overwhelmed?
3. Read Isaiah 40:12 (NIV): "Who has measured the waters in the hollow of his hand, or with the breadth of his hand marked off the heavens? Who has held the dust of the earth in a basket, or weighed the mountains on the scales and the hills in a balance?"
4. Discuss this verse with your spouse. What does it mean to you? What does it mean to be held by God?

Practical Application:

- Review your "to-do" list with your spouse. Discuss which items are priorities and which can wait, (e.g., spending quality time with your kids in the evening is more of a priority than washing the dinner dishes).

Prayer:

Father God, when I am overwhelmed, please help me remember to call on You—the One who can lift me higher than I can lift myself. Give me the courage and confidence to come to You, and leave unnecessary burdens behind. Amen.

WEEK 46: GROWING SPIRITUALLY WITH YOUR SPOUSE

*Therefore everyone who hears these words of
mine and puts them into practice is like a
wise man who built his house on the rock.
The rain came down, the streams rose, and
the winds blew and beat against that
house; yet it did not fall, because it had its
foundation on the rock. But everyone who
hears these words of mine and does not put
them into practice is like a foolish man
who built his house on sand. The rain
came down, the streams rose, and the
winds blew and beat against that house,
and it fell with a great crash.*

— MATTHEW 7:24-27 NIV

As your married life becomes more and more routine, some critical aspects of your relationship, once vibrant and growing, may start to fall by the wayside.

This is especially true of your spiritual growth! You may start strong, building a solid foundation of stone with great zeal and consistency at first... then, as daily life crowds in, you may lessen your times of prayer and Bible study... and before you know it, the basis of your marriage weakens.

Jesus spoke of two foundations: rock and sand.

We can build a solid foundation only when abiding by God's Word. It provides everything we need in order to survive the storms of life and remain steadfast through our own shortcomings, and those of our spouses. And, this is important: there is no other substitute.

Ecclesiastes 4:12 says that 'one may be overpowered, but two can defend themselves, and a strand of three is not quickly broken.'

While the Bible says two are better than one, it doesn't say marriage is easy. Both members must learn to stand against the enemy who may seek to overpower, but if they defend each other and their relationship with a strand of three—the husband, wife, and the Lord Jesus, they will be victorious.

And yet, partners will rarely share the same spiritual level, which calls for patience and loving endurance, as well as for consistent growth on both parts. One should not give up because the other is further along in Christ, nor should the one out front become discouraged and cut back on study and prayer.

Worship, study, and prayer in the home, and with other believers in a small group or church gathering, will encourage continuous growth. Furthermore, giving and serving together will help sharpen your spiritual gifts as you learn more about your partner in various settings. In addition, you may find inspiration from studying the lives of mature Christian couples from the past, especially those who served together in challenging situations such as the mission field, or during civil unrest.

Be determined to pray together and purposefully grow spiritually, and you'll enjoy a thriving marriage that's pleasing to the Lord, and nourishing for you and your spouse. Be the wise ones who build their house on the Rock of Christ Jesus.

Discussion Questions:

1. Do you regularly talk with your partner about the spiritual aspect of your relationship?
2. Are you both on the "same page" when it comes to spiritual growth?
3. Are there strategies you and your spouse have used to grow spiritually together? If so, write them down and discuss how they've helped your marriage.

Practical Application:

- Together, read Ephesians 4:14–15. Then, use this Scripture as a point of discussion with your spouse. How can the two of you set Jesus Christ apart as the ultimate commander of your marriage? What does it mean to grow toward Christian maturity (Rainey, 2000)?

Prayer:

Father God, I pray that You infuse us with the knowledge of Your will in all spiritual wisdom. Please help us grow toward Christian maturity in every way as we look to You, the Head of the Body. Amen.

WEEK 47: WIVES, SUBMIT TO YOUR HUSBANDS, HUSBANDS, LOVE YOUR WIVES

Submit to one another out of reverence for Christ. Wives, submit yourselves to your own husbands as you do to the Lord. For the husband is the head of the wife as Christ is the head of the church, his body, of which he is the Savior. Now as the church submits to Christ, so also wives should submit to their husbands in everything. Husbands, love your wives, just as Christ loved the church and gave himself up for her.

— EPHESIANS 5:21-25 NIV

As we see in today's passage, submission is actually a primary function of the church.

In fact, we're commanded to submit to one another out of reverence for Christ. But, as this reference sets forward: who is submitting to who? Most Bible scholars say this pertains to members of the body of Christ.

Thus, should a man submit to his sister in the Lord but not his wife? And, should a woman submit to a brother in the Lord in addition to her husband? The following line is clear: "Wives, submit yourselves to your own husbands as you do to the Lord." And we understand: "Husbands, love your wives, just as Christ loved the Church..." But how does all this submission play out in the lives of believers?

The essence of submission is setting aside one's thoughts, ideas and opinions in favor of another's. This is something that regularly takes place in the body of Christ—brothers and sisters working together for the good of the kingdom of God will often submit to each other, and God's guidance and commands, in order to get the job done.

Marital submission is the same: a husband and wife working together to preserve the God-ordained institution of marriage.

Throughout history, it was believed that wives had to submit to *any* order coming down from their husbands, while husbands took great license with their demands, sometimes forgetting the "love your wives, just as Christ loved the Church" portion of the deal. When Christ, love, and the giving up of oneself are neglected, submission is reduced to servitude, and sometimes even a form of slavery.

Reread the above passages, noting the continuous references to Christ, Lord, and Savior. This is because submission, love, and leadership must be centered in Jesus, or else it'll find itself lacking scriptural foundation and holiness.

Wives can more readily submit to their husbands when their husbands first submit to Christ. And husbands can more easily love and give themselves up for their wives when their wives first submit to Jesus.

In essence, a husband can submit to his wife as his sister in the Lord, as appropriate—while a wife submits to her husband as her brother in the Lord, as well as her husband. However, the marital injunctions for love, submission and leadership take top priority.

Discussion Questions:

1. What misconceptions have you had or heard about "submission" in marriage?
2. Think about your own marriage; what current patterns do you think should change, in light of Paul's teachings concerning submission?

Practical Application:

- Wives, read 1 Peter 3:5 (NIV): "For this is the way the holy women of the past who put their hope in God used to adorn themselves. They submitted themselves to their own husbands."
- Husbands, read 1 Corinthians 11:1 (NIV): "Follow my example, as I follow the example of Christ."
- Discuss the meaning of both passages.
- What is required of a wife, in order for her to practice biblical submission?
- What is required for a husband in order for him to lead his wife and family?

Prayer:

Heavenly Father, I pray that I take the commands in Ephesians 5:25 seriously. Please help me understand the true meaning of submission, and love with a focus on Christ. Amen.

WEEK 48: THREE MEANINGFUL WORDS: "I AM SORRY"

Have mercy on me, O God, according to your
unfailing love; according to your great
compassion blot out my transgressions.
Wash away all my iniquity and cleanse me
from my sin. For I know my
transgressions, and my sin is always
before me.

— PSALM 51:1-3 NIV

Let's talk about apologizing.

Saying "I'm sorry" can often be very challenging, depending on the circumstances, yet all apologies should be viewed as victories for your marriage. When you hold onto your "rightness," it may seem like you've chalked up a personal win; but the truth is, you've lost, as far as your relationship is concerned.

Consider a discussion between two tired spouses.

It's the end of the day, and both would rather don their pj's and head to the couch than discuss an unexpected dental bill. But, they enter a discussion, and it starts to escalate. Why didn't the one check their insurance before having the work done, and why is the other so upset? Why are both now starting to raise their voices?

It's simple: They're both reacting to a surprise fact—in this case, the dental bill—and they're expressing their displeasure about the situation by taking it out on their spouse. At that moment, neither is thinking that the brewing emotional damages they're allowing to pass could be worse than the monetary charges they're facing, so they justify their frustrations. Who among them will come forward with an apology, so they can resolve the real issue?

In Psalm 51: 1-3, King David works through true repentance before God. First, he asks for mercy, and mentions God's unfailing love and great compassion, then requests that his sins be removed from God's record. Finally, he asks to be washed and cleansed from his transgressions, which were always on his mind.

When we're genuinely sorry, we desire to learn from our mistakes, not to repeat them. In Psalm 51:10-12 (NIV), David asks God to restore their relationship: "Create in me a pure heart, O God, and renew a steadfast spirit within me. Do not cast me from your presence or take your Holy Spirit from me. Restore to me the joy of your salvation, and grant me a willing spirit to sustain me."

David exemplified a changed heart and a new attitude about His walk with God. This was necessary for the Lord to come in and complete the work of restoration. Had David held back with a half-hearted confession, or not turned away from his sin, cleansing and renewal would not have happened.

Be sure to use the three key little words: "I am sorry," when you hurt your spouse or children with your tone, or find you were wrong in placing blame. And, be more careful the next time, as such humility will model genuine sorrow and repentance, which has power to impact relationships inside and outside the home, and improve people's walk with God.

Discussion Questions:

1. Think of a time when someone apologized to you. How did it make you feel?
2. When was the last time you prayed to God to change your heart, or to give you a different perspective?
3. Have you ever hurt someone and felt sorry? What did God want you to learn from that situation?

Practical Application:

- Read Proverbs 18:17 (NIV): "In a lawsuit the first to speak seems right, until someone comes forward and cross-examines." Use this scripture as a talking point. What message can you glean here on how to handle your own shortcomings?

Prayer:

Heavenly Father, I humbly accept the mistakes I've made and come to You for repentance. I ask that You work through me, so I'll be quick to apologize to my spouse, and model what true repentance really looks like for my kids. Amen.

WEEK 49: NURTURING A LIFELONG FRIENDSHIP WITH YOUR SPOUSE

One who has unreliable friends soon comes to ruin, but there is a friend who sticks closer than a brother.

— PROVERBS 18:24 NIV

Nurturing a lifelong friendship with your spouse takes lots of time, attention, practice, prayer, faith, patience, and love—on an ongoing basis. If it seems like an impossible task, take courage, because life with your best friend is worth the effort.

Even if your friendship has to take a backseat to schedules, children, running the house, and other necessary distractions, you can still make the most of your time together in small moments.

C. S. Lewis said: "Friends look in the same direction."

That could mean working on the same projects, sharing the same dreams and goals, or working in the same ministry. Think about the verse from Proverbs—are you a reliable partner looking in the same direction as your spouse? Or are you looking off someplace else?

When you look away from your spouse, it can lead to a misunderstanding, or even all-out disaster. However, when both of you look to the Lord, your shared gaze in the right direction will ensure the health and safety of your marriage, and friendship. Who is it that sticks closer than a brother? This description of Christ Jesus is rooted in His selfless love and faithfulness, in a love that laid down His life for His friends.

Although your marriage will see many seasons of growth and change, these should serve to strengthen your bond with each other, and to God, who always sticks close. As you allow the love of God to saturate your hearts, you'll build deeper connections and trust for each other, which gives you an advantage over the lies of the enemy.

Ecclesiastes 4:9 says that "two are better than one." This speaks of support, companionship, and teamwork. Do you know what's happening at your spouse's place of employment? Do you know their desires for personal growth, or what worries them most?

It's vital to invest emotional energy into your spouse.

However, you can do this only when you understand how they think, respond, or react in a given situation. This requires openness from both the husband and the wife. A spouse who isn't in touch with their own thoughts and feelings and is, therefore, uncommunicative, withholds the deepest levels of friendship from their partner.

When your friendship is a top priority, you may often need to let other things go, or switch them to the back burner, in favor of spending time together. Invite the Lord into these special times by sharing what He's showing you in your personal study and prayer time. And, remember to leave space for quiet reflection, reminiscing, and laughter—just between the two of you, working towards sticking ever closer as the years go by.

Discussion Questions:

1. What do you want for your marriage 5 to 10 years from now? What steps can you take now to bring your vision to light (Chitwood, 2012)?
2. Have you made room in your life to nurture that friendship with your spouse? What activities need to be deprioritized, in order to help cultivate and grow a God-centered friendship with your spouse (Chitwood, 2012)?
3. What does marriage to your best friend look like? What is God's part in its development?

Practical Application:

- Think about shared hobbies or pastimes you enjoy doing with your spouse, and plan to partake in one of those activities this week. Do not allow anything to interfere with your plans (Chitwood, 2012).

Prayer:

Heavenly Father, today I commit myself to building a friendship with my spouse as a top priority. Please show me how to nurture our relationship, so that we can continue to enjoy each other throughout the years. Amen.

WEEK 50: CONSISTENCY WITH GOD IN YOUR MARRIAGE

Remain in me, as I also remain in you. No branch can bear fruit by itself; it must remain in the vine. Neither can you bear fruit unless you remain in me.

— JOHN 15:4 NIV

How can consistency with God improve your marriage?

First, let's consider a marriage without Him. The husband and wife go about their daily work routines, household responsibilities, tending to the children, time with friends, and popping in and out of fellowship. They watch TV, see a movie now and then, and join in with coworkers recounting the news. Otherwise, they eat, sleep, shop, and maybe pursue a hobby.

Our fictitious couple has a very full life!

Yet, where do they take their worries and concerns? Where do they derive peace from? When do they practice gratitude for their spouse, children, home, and jobs? Where do they find instruction, or seek guidance, for the many areas they must navigate? And how do they live lives of obedience to God?

God is patient. He is kind, slow to anger, and abounding in love. However, He also desires to be in a relationship with His children. Imagine if the couple in the above scenario gave their spouse the same amount of time as they did God? Would their marriage experience true intimacy, and would it stand the test of time?

Sometimes, it's difficult for us to understand why the Creator of the universe desires fellowship with mere humans, and yet, as we look back to the Garden of Eden, we see that this was precisely His intent. After He provided Adam with a wife, He always stayed in the picture. Even when Adam and Eve decided to step away from His presence, He sought them and desired to carry on with building upon that relationship. Why? Because without Him, they would die twice: physically and spiritually!

Marriage isn't meant to fulfill your every need, and neither is busyness. God stands by patiently, knowing which needs and desires He has planted in each soul that only He can fulfill. When a couple leans into His resting place together, they find the most profound intimacy of all: that of the *soul*.

Husbands and wives who share only the physical aspects of life in terms of living in the same house, procreation, and having both names on a bank account, know nothing of God's intention for unity. Lack of consistent connection with Him will eventually kill even physical intimacy, while seeking after Him, in contrast, will provide the most incredible closeness you and your spouse could ever imagine.

Discussion Questions:

1. What steps do you need to take in order to make your commitment to God a priority?

2. On a scale of 1 to 10, with 1 being not committed, and 10 being the highest level of commitment, how committed are you to the Lord? Why did you pick the number you did?

3. Are you as close to God as you would like to be? If not, what steps do you need to take to have a more consistent relationship with Him?

Practical Application:

- Together with your spouse, (and your age-appropriate children), schedule a recurring event on your calendar for prayer. You can set an alert on your cell phone or computer as a reminder. Make it a commitment with your family to spend more time in God's Word, and in

His presence, remembering all the benefits that you all stand to gain in doing so.

Prayer:

Father God, sometimes our lives get hectic and chaotic, and challenges arise that try to derail us from spending consistent time with You. We pray for Your power to stay focused, and remain faithful in our devotional time and in Your service. Amen.

WEEK 51: COMMITMENT FOR A LIFETIME

Haven't you read," he replied, "that at the
beginning the Creator 'made them male
and female,' and said, 'For this reason a
man will leave his father and mother and
be united to his wife, and the two will
become one flesh?' So they are no longer
two, but one flesh. Therefore what God has
joined together, let no one separate.

— MATTHEW 19:4-6 NIV

You stood there at the altar, or under the canopy, or on the
beach under a full moon, looking into the eyes of your partner,
while an official said something like this: "Before God, and this
company, do you take this man/woman to be your lawfully

wedded husband/wife; to have and to hold from this day forward, for better or for worse, for richer or for poorer, in sickness and in health; to love, honor and cherish, and forsaking all others, do you promise to be faithful to them as long as you both shall live?"

Then, with a heart full of love, hope, and excitement, you answered: "I do."

Then came the kiss, the triumphant walk past your family and friends, and hours of celebration. You were married. You legitimately belonged to each other, exclusively and forever. Then came the work of living out your pledge.

The promise to love and stick together no matter what may come is reflective of God's relationship with His children. Never does He wish to be apart from the objects of His love. Thus, it's never Him who chooses separation, even in eternity.

When Jesus spoke the famous words: "Therefore what God has joined together, let no one separate," He spoke an earthly proclamation to exemplify a heavenly principle.

The three biblical aspects of marriage include the following: oneness, faithfulness, and intimacy. Notice, however, that these three values pertain only to the relationship between husband and wife. Oneness in the flesh, faithfulness that excludes all others, and intimacy shared in sacred spaces. No other relationship on earth contains these elements (Crump, 2013).

Oneness, faithfulness, and intimacy are easily seen in the unity of the Trinity, and a marriage functioning in obedience and reverence for God reflects the unity of His image.

God was the silent and unseen officiant on your wedding day, presiding over the union of a man and a woman. When husband and wife continue to revere Him as the overseer of their marriage, they will live in peace, freedom, and security; steadfast and immovable when the enemy attempts to attack.

Esteem your marriage as an expression of God's plan for unity.

Although both man and woman are created in His image, equal in importance and function, neither alone is a complete reflection of His purposes on Earth. God desires for your marriage to endure, as His love endures, and to reflect His relational intentions, just as Christ did with His bride, the church.

Commitment for a lifetime to the same person is akin to commitment for a lifetime to the same God. Forsake all others and join together with your eyes on Him. When both partners hold themselves to "until death do us part," their marriage will be held in honor.

Discussion Questions:

1. Have you ever felt as if one of the three key values was lacking in your marriage? If so, what did you do to resolve the issue?

Practical Application:

- Together with your spouse, renew your wedding vows to each other. Use the traditional script above, or create your own, then read them aloud to each other (Crump, 2013).

Prayer:

Heavenly Father, thank You for my spouse. Help us remain committed to one another in this marriage based on Your purposes and principles. Amen.

WEEK 52: THE FAMILY THAT PRAYS TOGETHER STAYS TOGETHER

*But if serving the Lord seems undesirable to
you, then choose for yourselves this day
whom you will serve, whether the gods
your ancestors served beyond the
Euphrates, or the gods of the Amorites, in
whose land you are living. But as for me
and my household, we will serve the Lord.*

— JOSHUA 24:15 NIV

The most important life choice you will ever make, is your response to the following statement: "Choose for yourselves who you will serve."

Joshua was clear that there can be no compromise in our spiritual allegiance, and the Lord was emphatic in His statement: "I am the Lord God, who brought you out of the land of Egypt, out of the place of slavery. You shall have no other gods before me." (Exodus 20:2-3 NIV)

Joshua, through Moses, was well-aware of the preeminence of God, and His insistence that His children follow His instruction and align with His purposes for their own survival and spiritual wellbeing.

When Joshua made his commitment before the company of Israel, he encouraged everyone to make the right choice: to commit to obeying and trusting the One True God.

Prayer is the essential mode of connection with God in a Christian home. It directs each member toward a growing level of intimacy with the Lord, and introduces children to the mystery and excitement it provides.

Prayer also provides a practical demonstration of faith, which helps your children realize their relationship with their Heavenly Father. Prayers can be geared toward your children's immediate needs and be recorded in a family prayer journal. This provides a place to jot down requests, and fill in the answers, so everyone can experience the very real communion that God desires.

Prayers needn't be lengthy, complicated, or eloquent: the point of it all is a relationship with God, not adherence to religious formulas. If your family is just starting to walk with the Lord, prayer will help build a solid foundation that will see them grow in their relationship with Him in a steady and achievable way.

Help cultivate your children's awareness of God by speaking about the beauty of flowers, the shapes of clouds, and the softness of their puppy's fur.

Speak of the Lord in their presence before bedtime, during meals, and while on car rides. Use discussions about childish fears as opportunities to help your children get comfortable in the presence of God and learn to trust His love and protection.

As your children grow older, help them take their personal struggles to the Lord and draw their attention back to God when answers come: by thanking Him for what He's done.

Anyone who is determined to follow Christ, will play an integral part in influencing their present or future household in this most important decision: "As for me and my household, we will serve the Lord."

Discussion Questions:

1. Why is it important to pray together as a family?
2. In what ways can you incorporate prayer into your children's everyday lives?
3. How are you demonstrating your faith and your relationship with God in front of your children?

Practical Application:

- Pray the Lord's Prayer with your entire family, (Matthew 6:9-13). This is the prayer Jesus taught His followers to pray. Or, if your children are too young, have them pick a topic, and pray about it as a family. You can pray for the family, the kids, the world, or anything else they choose.

Prayer:

Father God, thank You for my wonderful family. I pray that You raise us up to be a family of prayer. May Your presence be fixed in our home, our hearts, and in all our affairs. Amen.

CONCLUSION

My Prayers for You and Your Family

An ever-growing, God-centered marriage is well within the grasp of any couple who prioritizes their walk with the Lord. He delights to match their every effort with His blessings, and provides step-by-step guidance in His Word.

If you wish to enhance the spiritual aspects of your marriage, you're in great company, and ready to embark on the next level. Live out what you have learned here, and pass along your experience to others longing to build godly marriages and families!

Focus on Christ, scripture, prayer, worship, fellowship, and relational health, in order to bring out the best in your spouse and children as you walk in His grace, and the power of His might. It is my prayer that this humble, yet insightful book of devotionals, will help you do just that.

If you found this book helpful and inspiring, please leave a review on Amazon, so that it may bless others in their pursuit of a lifelong, God-centered marriage! You'll be helping others find God's guidance for their lives, and hopefully receive His blessings and answers, as you have. In doing this, we can keep this circle of teaching and blessing going strong, and reach more and more hearts for the Lord to mend and heal—more families to restore with His timeless instructions and loving guidance.

Thank you for undertaking this journey, and may your family be ever more blessed in the Lord!

FROM ME, TO YOU!

A FREE GIFT TO OUR READERS

Claim your copy of "The 5 Most Costly Mistakes To Avoid In
Your Christian Marriage" to begin cultivating a God-centered
marriage starting now!

Scan the QR code below for access:

REFERENCE PAGE

Books:

Chapman, G. (1995). *The five love languages: How to express heartfelt*

commitment to your mate. Chicago, IL: Northfield Pub.

Websites:

Baby, R. (2020). *How to cope: Feeling guilty about not having more kids.* Regalo Baby.

https://regalo-baby.com/blogs/news/cope-feeling-guilty-not-kids

Baumer, G. Cortines, J. Wiggins, M. *God and money: Study guide chapter discussion questions. God and money.* https://static1.squarespace.-com/static/5511c272e4b0dc3ba763c0bc/t/

57c5b053893fc05eb474bd86/1472573523601/ChapterDiscus-sionQuestionsforGodandMoney.pdf

Chitwood, M. (2012). *Your spouse... your best friend?* Proverbs 31 Ministries.

https://proverbs31.org/read/devotions/full-post/2012/07/20/your-spouse-your-best-friend

Crump, L. (2013). *Couple devotional: Cherish your spouse.* Focus on the Family.

https://www.focusonthefamily.ca/content/couple-devotional-cherish-your-spouse

Crump, L. (2013). *Couple devotional: Healthy conflict management.* Focus on the

Family.

https://www.focusonthefamily.ca/content/couple-devotional-healthy-conflict-management

Crump, L. (2013). *Couple devotional: Lifelong commitment.* Focus on the Family.

https://www.focusonthefamily.ca/content/couple-devotional-lifelong-commitment

Crump, L. (2013). *Couple devotional: Positive communication*. Focus on the Family.

https://www.focusonthefamily.ca/content/couple-devotional-positive-communication

Crump, L. (2013). *Couple devotional: Time together.* Focus on the Family.

https://www.focusonthefamily.ca/content/couple-devotional-time-together

Eldemire, A. (2018). *4 key issues for new parents and how to solve them.* The Gottman

Institute.   https://www.gottman.com/blog/4-key-issues-new-parents-partner-solve/

Focus on the Family. (2016). *Marriage mentoring discussion guide.*

https://www.focusonthefamily.com/marriage/marriage-mentoring-discussion-guide/

Focus on the Family. (2011). *Praying together as a family.*

https://www.focusonthefamily.com/family-qa/praying-together-as-a-family/

Hawley, E. (2018). *God's marriage partnership plan.* Focus on The Family.

https://www.focusonthefamily.com/marriage/gods-marriage-partnership-plan/

Krejcir, R.J. (2003). *The character of flexibility*. Discipleship Tools.

http://www.discipleshiptools.org/apps/articles/?articleid=37152&columnid=4166

Kummer, T. (2011). *"Honor your father" bible lesson (exodus 20:12)*. Ministry to Children.

https://ministry-to-children.com/how-to-honor-your-father-lesson/

Lepine, B. (1999). *3 practical steps to biblical leadership in your home*. Family Life.

https://www.familylife.com/articles/topics/marriage/staying-married/husbands/3-practical-steps-to-biblical-leadership-in-your-home/

Michael, D. (2018). *The lord our god is with us*. Fighter Verses.

https://fighterverses.com/blog-post/lord-god-us-joshua-19/

Mowczko, M. (2010). *"Come to me"- A commentary on matthew 11:28-30*. Margmowczko.

https://margmowczko.com/come-to-me/

Northfield Publishing. (2021, July 15). *The love language quiz.* 5 Love Languages.

https://www.5lovelanguages.com/quizzes/

Prater, E. (2008). *Absorbing the initial shock of temporary separation.* Focus on the Family.

https://www.focusonthefamily.com/get-help/absorbing-the-initial-shock-of-temporary-separation/

Prater, E. (2008). *Dealing with physical distance in marriage.* Focus on the Family.

https://www.focusonthefamily.com/marriage/dealing-with-physical-distance-in-marriage/

Pugh, J. (2017). *Discussion guides: Biblical parenting.* Dare to Adventure.

https://daretoventure.org/biblical-parenting/

Rainey, D. (2000). *Walking with god in your marriage.* Family Life.

https://www.familylife.com/articles/topics/marriage/staying-married/growing-spiritually/walking-with-god-in-your-marriage/

The Holy Bible: New International Version. (2011). Bible Gateway.

https://www.biblegateway.com/versions/new-international-version-niv-bible/#copy. (Original work published in 1973)

Squires, J. (2016). *Marital intimacy is more than sex: Five ways to connect with your spouse.*

Desiring God. https://www.desiringgod.org/articles/marital-intimacy-is-more-than-sex

NOTES

_____

_____

_____

_____

_____

_____

_____

_____

_____

_____

_____

_____

_____

Made in the USA
Las Vegas, NV
06 May 2024